AMERICAN PROFILE

Here is a lively, penetrating, and provocative appraisal of American culture today, with special emphasis on art, theater, and television as well as individual morals, manners, and ideals.

With wit, wisdom and gentle irony, Louis Kronenberger, a brilliant critic, author and teacher, candidly analyzes the conflicts in our lives caused by our dual devotion to God and to Mammon. He boldly discusses the forces behind the commercialization of the arts, the wooing of middlebrow tastes in films and TV, the over-emphasis on specialized education, and deplores the desperate need for the solace of the analyst's couch in this urbane and revealing inquiry into contemporary American life.

"Full-packed, richly suggestive, imaginative . . . It's a stimulator . . . persuasive, witty and acutely perceptive . . ." *San Francisco Chronicle*

". . . absorbing subjects, all handled with a wit and couched in a style that, as H. L. Mencken used to say, should appeal 'to the civilized minority.' " *Cincinnati Times-Star*

". . . a toe-smashing, face-searing testament that rings as true as a silver dollar on marble . . . This book carries an Emersonian wallop." *Dallas Times Herald*

". . . written with grace and elegance . . . he cuts close to the bone and expresses many pointed truths." *New York Times*

THIS IS A REPRINT OF THE ORIGINAL HARDCOVER EDITION
PUBLISHED BY THE BOBBS-MERRILL COMPANY, INC.

Other MENTOR Books You Will Enjoy

AMERICA IN PERSPECTIVE (abridged)
Edited by Henry Steele Commager
Commentary on our national characteristics by 21
acute and perceptive foreigners from de Tocqueville to
Matthew Arnold and Denis W. Brogan. (#M30—35c)

HIGHLIGHTS OF MODERN LITERATURE: A Permanent
Collection of Memorable Essays from The New
York Times Book Review
Edited by Francis Brown
The world's leading authors and critics discuss modern
literature in fifty-eight informative, thoughtful and
stimulating articles from America's most influential
book section. (#M104—35c)

GOOD LISTENING (revised and up-dated)
by R. D. Darrell
Expert advice in the field of music and recording to
help you to increase your musical enjoyment and
widen your musical horizons. Includes a list of the
best LP recordings of the world's greatest music.
(#MD122—50c)

BALLET IN AMERICA *by George Amberg*
A survey of American ballet from early days of
theatrical dancing to the present, which includes two
original libretti by Jerome Robbins and Agnes de
Mille. Selected illustrations from the cloth-bound edition. (#MD123—50c)

AMERICAN ESSAYS (expanded)
Edited by Charles B. Shaw
A lively sampling of American thought from the 18th
century to the present: 34 superb essays by Franklin,
Emerson, Twain, Mencken, Lippmann, Highet, E. B.
White, and many others. (#MD137—50c)

TO OUR READERS

We welcome your comments about SIGNET, SIGNET KEY
and MENTOR Books as well as your suggestions for new
reprints. If your dealer does not have the books you want,
you may order them by mail, enclosing the list price plus
5c a copy to cover mailing costs. Send for a copy of our
complete catalog. The New American Library of World
Literature, Inc., 501 Madison Avenue, New York 22, N. Y.

COMPANY MANNERS

*A Cultural Inquiry
Into American Life*

BY
LOUIS KRONENBERGER

A MENTOR BOOK

Published by THE NEW AMERICAN LIBRARY

Published as a MENTOR BOOK
By Arrangement with The Bobbs-Merrill Company, Inc.

FIRST PRINTING, DECEMBER, 1955

MENTOR BOOKS are published by
The New American Library of World Literature, Inc.
501 Madison Avenue, New York 22, New York

PRINTED IN THE UNITED STATES OF AMERICA

To
Helen and Nathan Straus

"America is a 'happy-ending' nation."

—*From an address by* DORE SCHARY,
    Metro-Goldwyn-Mayer vice-president,
    to the Harvard Club of Los Angeles

AUTHOR'S NOTE

IN PRACTICE, this book attempts nothing like the scope its subtitle suggests: I can only plead that a really accurate subtitle would prove too wordy and unwieldy to serve as one. Actually this book is concerned only with such aspects of American life as I know something about—the professional and intellectual world, and the urban middle and upper-middle class. The book, again, nowhere tries to treat of great underlying forces, whether psychological, sociological, economic or religious; but only of cultural manifestations. Finally, though concerned with American beliefs and behavior, the book is perhaps at bottom as much a survey of an age as of a country. And though it is often sharply critical of our national faults, I would nowhere imply that they outweigh, in bulk, the faults of other nations. I simply know more, and care more, about them.

The Spirit of the Age and part of America and Art are reprinted by kind permission of The American Scholar.

CONTENTS

The Spirit of the Age

E VERY age looks at itself, compares itself with previous ages, and judges
itself on the basis of the comparison. That is how history
gets written, and that is why it keeps having to be rewritten;
for the age just before our own, in particular, always seems
almost glaringly wrongheaded. If an age is smug, and has
a Macaulay for its spokesman, it will regard all history as
a mere prelude to itself. But if, as is more often true, an
age is beset by doubts and bewildered by events, it will try,
rather, to see all history as an object lesson. The difficulty,
in every case, is to look at one's own time with objective
eyes and yet without assuming the privileges of posterity.
To try to disengage what seem the master traits of the age,
to try to find the main stream of one's period, its source
of flow and presumable destination—to try to find out these
things remains, surely, a kind of obligation, even if it be
treated a little as a game. Perhaps we tend to be wiser when
we do treat it a little as a game, for what might be called
the full-dress, or the hallowed and dedicated, search for
truth may well become too rigid and even self-righteous.
Truth, at any rate, has nothing whatever to do with sol-
emnity. And with most of us the wish to understand our
age is only part of the need to equilibrate ourselves, to
achieve some sort of working philosophy.

And part of looking at one's age means labeling one's
age—something that is at least as perilous as it is tempting.
For, naturally, you can no more epitomize a whole era than
you can indict a whole nation. You can't even bite into an
age as you do into an apple, for it has not the solid, or the
simple, or the unshifting qualities of an apple. But it may
have some traits whereby, like an apple, it bulges too much

11

on one side or is too ripe or too green; it may have traits that are unique; it *must* have—though there is no assurance that we can spot them—master traits. What are the striking, the special, the so-to-speak symbolic qualities of our time? What—if, indeed, manners makyth man— are our predominating manners? Wherein does 1954 differ from 1902 or 1854 or 36 B.C.? I shan't pretend to say; but I shall at least speculate.

From among many possible descriptive labels, I shall use but two; and one I shall borrow. Mr. Auden a few years ago spoke of our age as the Age of Anxiety. An age that may be said to have begun with the concept of the inferiority complex, and that vibrates angrily now with the menace of the H bomb, will hardly bring serenity. An age that saw a totalitarian regime bring on a catastrophic war, that has produced in turn further fighting and a barely nominal peace, is not likely to be an age of reassurance. It must be the cry of almost every age that it was born a little too late, or too soon. But the people of this age do have some cause for thinking that they have been assaulted and disrupted beyond the common measure. Freud—to go no farther—has forced them to have quite unprecedented and often highly unpleasant opinions about themselves, their fathers, their mothers, their wives, their children. The key figure of the age has been, of course, the psychoanalyst, who has not been a very well-understood figure, either. The general public has been led to regard him as a combination of priest and Pinkerton operative, so that the general public has been led to form romantically sinister opinions about him. The huge way in which he looms, moreover, is to this extent a liability: it is a reminder that we may be, each of us, far from well: the man who symbolizes the cure also emphasizes the ailment. No doubt he is there to tell us that we have nothing to fear but fear, but also to point out how many odd identities, how many artful disguises, fear can have. I am so far from optimistic about today's world or tomorrow's as to be hopelessly unsure where safety, let alone salvation, lies; but there is a form of pessimism that is part of our current psychology that I consider unfortunate. Most ages that aren't completely smug tend, after observing themselves, to run themselves down.

Hamlet is perhaps most neurotic, most modern, most time-less, for exclaiming "The time is out of joint." And if it is the great delusion of moralists to suppose that all pre-vious ages were less sinful than their own, then it is the great delusion of intellectuals to suppose that all previous ages were less sick. However shocking the pillage and murder statistics of the Middle Ages, we somehow see the inhabitants as heartily sustained by a faith in God. What-ever the excesses and pestilences of the Renaissance, we see its inhabitants as hale and whole through their faith in themselves. However incessant villainy may have been in the eighteenth century, or however endemic the vapors, we somehow see the Augustans as integrated and healthy through their faith in reason. Hence, though far from opti-mistic about today's world or tomorrow's, I suspect that lots of people in the Middle Ages or the Renaissance or the Enlightenment were quite as sick as ourselves.

Indeed, the Age of Reason might almost literally have been called the Age of Eccentrics. In the field of manners, it was the age when Chesterfield thought it vulgar to play the violin, and other aristocrats found it pleasant to watch people hanged. It was the age (if we can believe Samuel Rogers) when a lady remarked that her drawing room smelled of violets, and a gentleman replied, "Madam, that is me." It was the age when Porson, the greatest classical scholar in England, drank ink when he could not get wine, and when Admiral Byng, an hour before he was to be executed, "took his usual draught for the scurvy." Nor can we fail to note that during the Age of Reason thousands of people went painfully out of their wits at religious revival meetings; that during the Age of Reason, Swift went insane, Christopher Smart went insane, Collins went insane—and, for that matter, the King of England went violently insane. So that perhaps we, today, do not too greatly surpass all other eras in sickness of soul or mind. Beyond the fact that ours has been genuinely an age of crises, it is one of anxiety because we have begun to face unpleasant facts about ourselves and unpleasant facts about the universe. In the first flush of these revelations we tended to become more cynical and amoral, but equally to become more tolerant. The manners of the 1920s, complicated by that social phenomenon known as Prohibition, became rebellious by intent and unrepressed by circumstance: there seems to be a terrible misunderstanding on the part of a great many people to the effect that when you cease to believe you may cease to behave. The manners of the 1930s, complicated by that pressure known as Social Consciousness, became at once very doctrinaire and very careless: there were presumably no two ways of doing the things that mattered, and it did not matter how you did the rest. Yet the depression years of the '30s, plagued though they were by want and menaced though they were by war, were perhaps less an age of anxiety than this is, because the '30s felt that the coming explosion would be a thunderstorm to clear the air. Today the worst kind of perplexity is added to anxiety: the future, which a while back we were all plotting, however desperately, like a game of chess, has now become something we can only gamble on, like a game of roulette.

And this is, I think, very much the Age of Anxiety, the age of the neurosis, because along with so much that weighs on our minds there is perhaps even more that grates on our nerves. Has there ever been an age so rife with neurotic sensibility, with that state of near shudders, or near hysteria, or near nausea, much of it induced by trifles, which used to belong to people who were at once ill-adjusted and overcivilized? Has there ever before been such an assortment of people who have found such an assortment of things to set their teeth on edge? I am not speaking of the Horace Walpoles or the Hedda Gablers, the squeamish exquisites or frustrated neurotics who inhabit every age. Most people of breeding have always been "jarred" by clashing colors, or scratchy pens, or rasping voices: they were neurotic, that is, to the degree that they were "aesthetic." But now, and by the thousands, and with no assurance whatever that the edgier the teeth the more *raffiné* the taste, people are quirky, jumpy, jittery, inwardly tense. And since, in far too many cases, we cannot set this down to their being overbred, we can only conclude that they are overburdened. They are reacting to the pressures of a world, in itself insecure, with too aggressive techniques.

Physically, mechanically, modern life is on the whole a very superior mode of existence. It is noisy, very noisy in big cities, but it has always been very noisy in big cities; the rumble of moving carts, the din of street criers and bell ringers during the seemingly idyllic times assaulted the ear quite as unpleasantly as honking horns and screaming sirens and blasting and riveting today. Life is dirty, very dirty in big cities, but consider the coal smoke and exposed garbage of past times, not to speak of the days when housewives poured their slops out of upstairs windows, and ditches choked with dead dogs and refuse ran down the middle of the streets. Consider the stenches that were ubiquitous for centuries and have been outlawed, really, only in our own time. Most of all, consider how much better our nerves *should* be, living as we do in an age of comparative courtesy. It is true that the high breeding and distinguished manners of a small special class have all but vanished and that ours is an age of extremely sloppy behavior. But it is not what most past periods have been—ages of extremely arrogant, of appallingly rude, behavior. The Augustan Age that boasts a reputation for perfect breeding and supreme urbanity was in general the most highhanded, quarrelsome, insulting, slanderous, straight-out downright rude age—rude to the point of being brutal, rude to the point of being cruel—that one could well conceive. We all remember Alexander Pope's magnificent abusiveness; what we may have forgotten is how harshly he could be abused.

On the other hand, we can hardly not put in evidence that archfoe of stability and serenity—speed; we can hardly doubt that all the rush, the hurry, the headlongness of life has told on our nerves in America. It is not a difference in passion, any more than a difference in plumbing, that really distinguishes our life from that of our ancestors; it is a difference in pace. We not only travel faster than we used to, in subways rather than sedan chairs, in planes rather than on horseback. We eat much faster than we used to; we talk much faster than we used to—so much that the drawl, which once we thought rather charming, is nowadays apt to set those aforementioned teeth on edge. Certainly we get bored and blasé much faster than we used to: we have lost much of the wide-eyed interest in things

that earlier ages had, but even more we have lost their
capacity to *remain* absorbed. The public that waited from
month to month in a pleasurably wild suspense for the new
installment of a novel by Richardson or Dickens, and
waited with such intensity that the matter of Clarissa Har-
lowe's virtue became something like a national crisis—
such a public remains incomprehensible to us who, in the
same space of time, would more likely encounter Clarissa in
a magazine serial, as a novel between covers, as a *Reader's
Digest* abridgement, as a movie, as a musical, as an opera,
as a ballet, as a comic strip, as a play—and very possibly as
a plagiarism.

And what counts more in this age of anxiety than our
eating or talking or traveling or tiring of things faster than
we used to is the fact that we now succeed or fail much
faster than we used to. Fame was once built like furniture
—slowly, painstakingly, expensively; but then it lasted a
lifetime. Once people did not simply read novels, they
read novelists; the new Meredith or Hardy, even the new
Wells or Mrs. Wharton, was a kind of obligation even
when it failed to be an event. People were faithful to their
matinee idols during half a lifetime; they grew old, indis-
solubly bound to Julia Marlowe or John Drew, as one
grows old with one's wife or one's husband, for better for
worse, for richer for poorer. Today the few bobby-soxers
who are not shamelessly fickle are flagrantly polyandrous.
Byron had, of all writers, the most dazzlingly meteoric rise
to fame, and even Byron was left a little breathless by
waking up one morning to find himself famous. But on
any morning these days whole segments of the population
wake up to find themselves famous, while, to keep matters
shipshape, whole contingents of celebrities wake up to find
themselves forgotten. Consider only that portion of the
population that has not yet attained the age of twelve.
There was a time, and a fairly recent one, when you could
probably count on the fingers of one hand all the famous
people in the world under the age of twelve: a musical
child prodigy like Hofmann or Elman, a ten-year-old boy
at Harvard, a boy king, a child princess, a Daisy Ashford
or a Charley Ross. Now we have movie children who
earn a million dollars before you can say Jack Robinson

or they can say cat; we have little Quiz Kids and other prodigies of every description, many of them past their peak at nine and all washed up at fourteen.

Yet the comic and satiric aspects of all this, beyond being themselves a little crude, must give way before the real implication of such rocketing success and plummeting failure. Certainly in these days success is almost without distinction, as failure is without dignity; certainly, too, success must leave one quite as anxious as failure. For how much pride is to be had in the winning, and how much permanence goes with what is won? The technique of winning is so shoddy, the terms of winning are so ignoble, the tenure of winning is so brief; and the specter of the has-been—a shameful rather than a pitiable sight today— brings a sudden chill even to our sunlit moments.

Among many other slogans that might partly express the spirit of the age I would add to Mr. Auden's just one of my own—and one at the strict level of manners, which of course his is not. The perturbations of our time go far deeper than the mores know how to explain. But on the surface of life, where we can only guess at times how sick people are by how strangely they act, or infer their anxieties from their absurdities, perhaps our age is more than anything else the Age of Publicity. In terms of affecting our lives today, I think the only man fit to be compared with Sigmund Freud or Karl Marx is P. T. Barnum. After Barnum, life was to have all the charlatanry of the old-time circus, though much less of the charm. After him, it would be folly to think that good wine needs no bush. After him, things that had customarily been done for pleasure were to be done for pay; after him, there was to be less and less privacy in life, and so less and less feeling that privacy is a desirable thing. After Barnum came the press agent and the stooge, the chatter column, the gossip columnist; and Oscar Wilde's remark that there is one thing worse than being talked about and that is not being talked about became more and more true as it became more and more trite. After Barnum—two or three generations after Barnum—people were married at the top of Ferris wheels, and spent their wedding nights in department-store show windows, and gave birth to children under klieg lights, and threw tremendous parties to celebrate their divorce. For Barnum had triumphed, ballyhoo had triumphed, at any rate in America; and with it we have seen something not so much vanish as become tawdry and besmirched. Along with Barnum's celebrated cynicism about the birth rate there was his humor about, say, the Grand Egress; there was his vitality, his sense of the gaudy, his knack for the unexpected. And all this has persisted into our own time, and we still offer our own version of it today—dressing up celebrities, dressing up nonentities, in anything from adjectives to leopard skins. And we do it all in a style to prove that there is still plenty of slapdash color in American life, still plenty of energy and ingenuity and exuberance. The trouble with us in America isn't that the poetry of life has turned to prose, but that it has turned to advertising copy.

And in an age of publicity, technique becomes all-important: the proper presentation, as the advertising world describes it; the proper packaging, as the mercantile world describes it; the phrase that will linger; the face you won't forget. Philistia, furthermore, swallows it all, loves it, imitates it. A man named Turner recently told me he had named his baby son Tommy, not as you might suppose because the alliteration pleased him, but because "Tommy Turner" is an easy name to remember and "that would prove very useful in business." But the very publicity that dictates our habits destroys our thinking. For the great conspiracy of our time is that nobody shall be forced, shall even be permitted, to learn the truth about anything, or the beauty or value of anything, *at first hand:* that we shall all be veritable kings in the sense that we have tasters, and veritable princelings in the sense that we have whipping boys; and that people couldn't be more willing to do our reading for us if we were blind; or more eager to cut up our culture into little pieces for us if we were babies. The directions for becoming cultured are, as it were, right on the box and are as simple and plain as the directions for baking a cake. The wonder of our age is that everything is labeled and spotlighted, preshrunk, predigested, passed on by experts. The trouble with our age is that it is all signposts and no destination.

It would be worse than naive, of course, to tax the age with originating all this. It is much more a matter of degree. A certain veneration of the limelight is as old as human vanity, and the remark "You go not to see but to be seen" has been traced as far back as Socrates and Xanthippe and might well be traced much farther. All the same, the spectacle of a fashionable first-night theater audience, with its repulsive knowingness, its nonchalant exhibitionism, its ability, in the lobby before the curtain goes up, to be as warm and gushing as a geyser; and in the theater after the show has started, to be as cold and crushing as a glacier—all this seems to be quite as much a phenomenon of our own time as it is a manifestation of a theater that is dead—or, more accurately, a theater that repulses most things that are alive.

Plainly, again, there were Men of Distinction acting as decoy ducks in the pleasure gardens and spas of two centuries ago; and the Art of Puffing was far advanced before the press agent had been born, or at any rate christened. Yet, in the old days, all this was of small bore, short of range, and went off with not too loud a report. Ours is pre-eminently an age of publicity because it is so well equipped to publicize: one advertising agency, one radio or TV station can do in a day what once upon a time took months. And with everything publicized so nimbly, and packaged so smartly, and swallowed so painlessly, the outer sophistication is greater today, the enameling is smoother. No doubt people of taste and sensibility always think that their age is pre-eminently vulgar; and so is ours. Yet we may wonder whether, in the primary sense, this is so true of our own time; we can hardly help noticing that what might be called a pristine vulgarity is largely outlawed, largely gone. Gone is the worst of the Gilded Age, as expressed in mere Bigness and Muchness and Thickness and Richness and Newness. It was too oppressive, too indigestible. We have invented streamlining, and we have learned to put our faith in the specialist. The Age of the Specialist is folded into the Age of Publicity and could hardly exist outside it. Ours is not so much an age of vulgarity as of vulgarization; everything is tampered with or touched up, or adulterated or watered down, in an effort to make it palatable, in an effort to make it pay.

What we need for cultural health today is what we needed and got for our physical health nearly half a century ago: Pure Food & Drug Laws concerning thought and feeling. But it is very much a question whether we shall get them. The problem in any case—even divorcing it from the far vaster one of world politics and economics—the problem in the realm of manners, on the plane of culture, is immensely difficult, involving as it does all the impurity, the pull-two-ways by which we live and by which we have perhaps immoderately prospered. It might be more horrifying, but it would be far simpler, if America were completely soulless and visionless, were altogether materialistic. It is a good deal more complicated because we are of so mixed a composition, so bifocal an outlook, serving God and Mammon both, and both at the same time.

ONE

1. America and Art

1

THE compelling fact about art in America is that it is not organic. It has almost no share in shaping our life; it offers, rather, compensation for the shapelessness. And just because we prescribe a certain amount of art for ourselves as a kind of corrective—being "deficient" in art as we might be in calcium or iron—we regard it less as ordinary nourishment than as a tonic, something we gulp rather than sip, regard with esteem and yet suspicion, and either require to be made up with a pleasant taste or exult in because it tastes unpleasant. The American feeling, or lack of feeling, for art has been immemorially easy to satirize, whether at the one extreme of Babbittry or at the other of Bohemia. All the same, for whatever reasons, such feeling has long been part of the American character—which is to say that the American bent, the American genius, has honestly moved in other directions. Like the Romans and the Germans, we are not an artistic people. This may be partly the result of our so long being able to reach out, rather than having to turn inward; of our possessing a vast continent to traverse, subdue, explore, develop, grow rich on, so that there was no husbanding or skilled handling of resources, no modifying what we started with or were saddled with into something gracious and expressive. A race, like an individual, develops a style in part through what it has uniquely, in part through what it has too little of. French prose owes its dry, neat lucidity to the same things that produced a general lack of magic in French poetry; French women owe their chic, I would think, to their general lack of girlish beauty. Americans have suffered from over-abundance—from not needing to substitute art for nature, form for substance, method for materials. At the very point where a patina might begin to appear, or mellow-ness to suffuse, we have abandoned what we made for something newer, brisker, shinier; and with each such act we have become a little less "artistic" in our approach. But of course there is more to it than that. An artistic people—the French, the Chinese, the ancient Greeks—is one whose necessities are made the comelier by its dreams, but whose dreaming is equally controlled by its necessi-ties: the two are integrated, are never so harshly at odds that the dreaming must serve as a lurid compensation. With an artistic people a kind of good sense regulates both its acquisitive side and its aspiring one; and from deprecating excess on a large scale, it eventually does so in small ways as well. Hence the design of existence stands forth more powerfully than the décor; and because design, unlike décor, affects a whole society, the national traits and in-stincts and responses get beyond cost or size or class, and equally characterize the rich and the poor, the cultivated and the unlettered. There is always a sense of bone struc-ture about an artistic people—think of the Spaniards—a touch of severity, of economy. There is, I suppose, some-thing rather classic than romantic—a sense of the ancestor as well as the individual.

An artistic people need not (and very likely will not) be profoundly poetic or mystical, as the English and the Germans are. It is plainly because the English and the Germans lead such double lives, because one extreme must almost atone for the other, because dreaming grows out of repressions or helps to stamp out reality, that two nations so given to vulgar instincts and material aims should be capable of such splendid intensities—intensities which, for all that, do constitute excesses. And we too, as a people, are driven to compensate; are so excessively aspiring for being so excessively acquisitive; come back to God through guilt or satiety; go on binges with Beauty because it is no part of our daily life—and we somehow think the extent of the undertaking will make up for the quality. Our magnates are always giving away millions not too shiningly acquired; our aging plutocrats leave a spendthrift order for art like the flashy sports who buy their women ten dozen American Beauty roses. Nothing amuses or appalls us more than a gangster's funeral with its carloads of flowers and wreaths; and nothing teaches us less. The gangster's funeral is actually the model for Broadway's supermusicals, for the murals on civic architecture, for Florida's luxury resorts; and the gangster's funeral is itself a late development, the descendant of the Newport "cottage"—the only difference being that at Newport conspicuous waste was confined to living, where in Chicago it specialized in death.

But it is not just the excesses born of wealth that have failed to make us an artistic people. After all, corsairs and conquistadors are the ancestors of *most* cultures; and French chateaux and Italian *palazzi* of even the best periods stress sheer display quite as much as they stress beauty. We may just come near enough to being an artistic people to explain why we *are* not and perhaps *cannot be* one. We are an inventive and adaptive people; and thus our whole effort, our whole genius, is to modify rather than mold, to make more efficient rather than more expressive. We are dedicated to improvement—to improving our minds and our mousetraps, our inventions and our diets. We are so dedicated to improvement that we neither ask nor care whether a thing needs to be improved, is able to be improved, or, qualifying as an improvement, will necessarily seem a benefit. We never seem to wonder whether we may not be complicating things by simplifying them, or making them useless by so constantly making them over. But the ability to invent, the desire to improve, may partly spring from our having got so much later a start than other civilizations—from our being at a log-cabin and homespun stage when Europe had long achieved silks and marble, and then lagging for so long behind them. We first were made competitive from a sense of our marked inferiority to others; we then became, from our sense of our natural wealth and resources, competitive among ourselves; and we are now, of course, inventive *because* we are competitive: last year's model must be disparaged so that this year's model can be sold. But no matter how genuine was the original impulse, or how sheerly commercial it is today, inventiveness has become ingrained in our practice, and our source of constant pride; and even among the best of us—unless we are extremely vigilant—it is now an influence on our taste. Abroad, avant-gardism expressed the crying need among old cultures for new forms and feelings; here, we often seem to be breaking with tradition before establishing it; here, experiment has a gadget air, a will-to-invent about it, as often as a sense of rebellion or release.

This gadget aspect crops up everywhere, in the most unexpected places. Thus our highbrow criticism is constantly inventing and amending a vocabulary—one that somehow will seem a special, up-to-the-minute possession for critics, exactly as the latest models in cars or television sets will seem a special, up-to-the-minute possession of prosperous businessmen. The actual character, too, of our present-day literary jargon—so much of it psychiatric and sociological—is that of a profoundly inartistic, indeed, an aesthetically quite barbarous, yet irrepressibly inventive people. Take just one simple example. In the entire language I doubt whether there exists an uglier word, or one less needed for the use it has been put to, than the word *sensitivity*. One special and particular meaning could be allowed it—the sensitivity, let us say, of a photographic plate to light. But even among critics with a historical sense and a cultivated ear, it has almost completely ousted the two words that for centuries so happily shouldered, and so neatly divided, the burden: *sensibility* and *sensitiveness*. But the whole highbrow vocabulary, the whole need for new spring-and-fall models in literary language—*subsume* one year, *mystique* the next, *exfoliate* the year after—exhibits our national need to adapt and amend and apply at any cost, with no great concern for the urgency, and perhaps even less for the rightness, of the words themselves. And even more indicative than their original "coinage" is the indecent speed with which they become almost unbearable clichés; even more, also, than their coinage itself is the fact that they are so uniformly pretentious, so very rarely picturesque. If only critics would read Dr. Johnson for his wisdom and not for his unhappier choices in words. We are inartistic, indeed, in our very approach to art.

We have never as a people regarded art as something to live with, to freely delight in, to call by its first name. Perhaps this derives from something beyond an inventive streak that keeps us restless, or an awe that makes us uncomfortable: perhaps had we had more opportunity to live with art, we might have acquired a more relaxed attitude toward it. It has never been on our doorstep; we have had to go in search of it, go doubly in search—as much to discover what it is as where it is. The journeys have had a little of the air of pilgrimages; the works of art, a great deal of the sanctity of shrines. The whole burden of our criticism, our constant cultural plaint, is how scant, and impure, and imperfect, and isolated, art in America has been—which, inevitably, has conditioned our approach to it. We insist on strong, emphatic, unmistakable reactions; we either swoon or snub, analyze at tedious length or dismiss with a mere wave of the hand. We go at art, in other words, not like casual, cultivated shoppers, but like a race of antique-shop dealers for whom everything is either magnificently authentic or the merest fake; and the result—though of course there are other reasons, too—is that we cannot take art in our stride. So belated and uneasy an approach has made us about art what Prohibition made my whole generation about wine: either frank, unblushing ignoramuses or comically solemn snobs. Different levels of Americans reveal very different attitudes toward art; but what is perhaps most significant is that they all reveal one marked kind of attitude or another. They either tend to hold back lest they commit howlers; or to go into raptures lest they be taken for clods; or to pooh-pooh the whole business lest they seem longhaired and sissified; or to purse their lips and utter pronunciamentos lest they seem just vulgarly susceptible or humanly responsive.

If classifying them as fence-straddlers or as poseurs or as philistines or as prigs is to simplify and even travesty the matter, it may yet help account for the fact that we are not a people for whom, at any level, art is just a natural and congenial aspect of existence. The very "uselessness" of it—the fact that art, like virtue, is its own reward; again, the very magic of it—the fact that it cannot be reduced to a formula or equation; the utter arrogance of it—the fact that money cannot buy it nor American salesmanship or elbow grease achieve it: these are, at the very outset, reasons for mystification and distrust. *Its* kind of arrogance, of refusal to be won on extrinsic terms—as of a high-mettled, beautiful girl whom no suitor can win on the strength of his bank account, his family background, or his sober, industrious habits—seems improper, even unethical, to a people who can respect putting a high price on something, who can approve and even enjoy a hard tussle till things are won, but who can no more understand than they can approve that something is beyond negotiations, is just not to be bought. Art to their minds is not a high-mettled girl, but an extremely unreasonable woman. Art's kind of magic again — art's refusal to be achieved through laboratory methods, through getting up charts or symposiums or sales conferences, through looking at smears under the microscope—its magic seems behind the times, almost downright retarded, to a people with a genius for the synthetic. Art's kind of uselessness, finally—its non-vitamin-giving health, its non-pep-you-up modes of pleasure, its non-materialistic enrichment—quite genuinely confuses a people who have been educated to have something to show for their efforts, if only a title or a medal or a diploma. Art, for most Americans, is a very queer fish—it can't be reasoned with, it can't be bribed, it can't be doped out or duplicated; above all, it can't be cashed in on.

Someone, Max Beerbohm perhaps, once defined a Bohemian as a person who uses things for what they're not intended—a window drapery, let us say, for a ball dress, or a goldfish bowl for a soup tureen. And this just a little defines the American sense of the artistic. We must endow everything with a new twist, an added value, an extra function. We literally cannot let well enough alone; hence we

very often make it worse—and never more, perhaps, than
when we also make it better. The new element, the new
effect, the new use to which an art form is put, very often
has to do with achieving something more tractable or
palatable or painless or time- or labor-saving; with offering, at the very least, old wine in new bottles, and much
more to our satisfaction, old wine in plastic containers or
ice cream cones. Thus we have Somerset Maugham re-edit
and abridge the classics; we get a present-day version of
Buckingham's *The Rehearsal,* a Negro *Juno and the Pay-*
cock, a *Cherry Orchard* laid in Mississippi; we have Mr.
Orson Welles telescoping five of Shakespeare's plays into
one; we have something written for the piano performed
on the violin, something intended for men taken over by
women. We're not, to be sure, the only nation that does
such things, but I think we're the only nation that feels a
compulsive urge to do them. Where the Germans have a
particular genius for ersatz, for substitutions, we have one
for new twists and gimmicks, new mixtures and combina-
tions. We simply *have* to tamper: if we don't cut the words,
we must add to the music; if we don't change the story,
we must shift the locale. Nowhere else, surely, can there
be such a compulsion to make plays out of books, musicals
out of plays, *Aida's* into *My Darlin' Aida's;* to insert scenes,
delete characters, include commentators; to turn gas sta-
tions into cathedrals, or churches into dance halls. Out of
Plato and Berkeley we get Transcendentalism; out of Transcendentalism we concoct Christian Science; and then, almost immediately, Jewish Science out of Christian. Many
nations have discovered the devil in dancing, but we are
perhaps the first to find God through calisthenics.

And no doubt we create, from all this, the illusion that
we are notably experimental in the arts, ever seeking new
forms, contriving new functions, establishing new per-
spectives. But, even ignoring the material or commercial
side of it all, our contrivance of so many artful blends and
twists and variants is really our avoidance of art itself,
exactly as our craving for sensations argues a distaste or
fear of experiences. Our whole artistic effort, if it does
not parallel, at least involves our genius for concocting
the mixed drink and for putting the packaging ahead of

the product. The result—from which almost all of us suffer more than we realize—is a kind of vulgarization, and one that can take place at high levels no less than at low ones. Our stressing significance in art rather than intensity, our present search for symbolic figures and concealed meanings and multiple levels: isn't this part of our compulsion to introduce something new, add something extra, offer something unprecedented? Does it not bear witness, also, to our intellectual ingenuity rather than our aesthetic responsiveness? Hasn't the new multi-level *Pierre* or *Confidence Man* a kinship with the new split-level house, or the concealed meanings with the concealed plumbing, or the indirect approach with the indirect lighting, or the taste for knotty problems with the taste for knotty pine? I do not think I am being anti-intellectual when I say that in America the intellect itself is being overused and misused in the world of art, where—after all—the most thoughtful elucidation avails nothing without the right, pure, instinctive response; for in art the reverse of Wordsworth's saying is also true and immensely important: in art, there are tears that do often lie too deep for thoughts.

Given our inventiveness, such endless and manifold vulgarization is inevitable. No race can make an idea go farther than we can. We get the last ounce of derivable income from it; we carry it, indeed, to distances that virtually obscure the original starting point. From the classic sandwich made with bread we evolve the triple-decker made with ice cream; from the first motel, that could hardly have competed with a bathhouse, we are now contriving structures that will outdo—if not soon outmode—the Ritz. And quite beyond our double-barreled desire to make things profitable as well as attractive, all this technical skill and inventive cleverness must in the end conspire as much against our creative instincts as against our artistic ones. A nation that can so marvelously concoct must less and less feel any need to create. We are developing a genius for rewrite at the expense of one for writing, for stage directors who shall do the work of dramatists, for orchestrators who shall do the work of composers. Everything today must carefully and exactly conform to public taste, yet offer a new wrinkle into the bargain—we insist on what might be called a kind of Murphy-bed of Procrustes.

The effect of this vulgarization is almost sure to be pervasive and permanent. There is something disarming, often indeed unnoticeable, about vulgarization itself. Sheer vulgarity quickly stands self-condemned, hence tends quickly to correct itself. Or where it persists—as representing something congenial to a particular social milieu or human type —it is so blatant as to isolate itself and proclaim its own quarantine. So long as what is "wrong" can be quickly spotted, and thereafter vividly contrasted with what is "right," whether or not it continues to exist, it can no longer triumph. The most insidious aspect of vulgarity, I would think, concerns not those to whom its appeal is obvious and immediate, but those, rather, whom it gradually and imperceptibly manages to win over, those who in the beginning are partly superior to it and who only by habituation sink to its level. A vulgarity that can thus contaminate won't often, it seems clear, be of a primitive or glaring sort; it will be, rather, a worm in the apple, a sort of Greek bearing gifts. In the world of art, such vulgarity may boast that it does far more good than it does harm, that it makes many people respond to what they might otherwise pass by. I'm not speaking of the out-and-out popularization, but rather of such things as the movie version of *Henry V* or Stokowski's arrangements of Bach— of things offered under the auspices of culture and aimed at reasonably cultured people. This form of vulgarization will by no means altogether misrepresent or even too greatly discolor. And though a severe taste may resist or reject it at once, a fairly sensitive taste—what I suppose is most conveniently called a middlebrow taste that, if left alone, might come to appreciate Bach or Shakespeare "neat"— will not resist or reject the adulteration, will soon, in fact, come to prefer and eventually to require it.

Vulgarization isn't always a matter of making things pleasanter to the taste, or easier to swallow; it can also consist—which can constitute the highbrow maneuver—in making them more difficult and abstruse, rather resembling the homely girl who goes out of her way to accentuate her homeliness. It is as possible to defeat the primary end of art, the sense of beauty, by minimizing it as by rouging it up. Short cuts represent one kind of vulgarization, labyrinths represent another. The highbrow procedure, if we were to raid the vocabulary that accompanies it, might be called countervulgarization. It constitutes, in any case, no cure or corrective for the middlebrow ailment, but rather a different kind of disease; and though its very lack of cheap allure will cause it to render art far less of a disservice than the rouge-and-syrup process, it is yet equally a barrier to our becoming an artistic people. What with art being something, on the one side, that slides smoothly down our gullets and, on the other, something to be chewed long after any flavor is left, we can seldom any longer, I think, get the fine, sharp, vivid, simple first experience of art that must be the preliminary to any more complex one. Something is always doused over it or drained out of it, hiding the flavor or heightening it, removing gristle or adding lumps; or the thought or look of the thing, before we even bite into it, conditions us. A man can no longer even read, let us say, the "Ode to a Nightingale" without the slightly guilty or, at any rate, self-conscious feeling that it is "romantic poetry."

As a result of the vulgarizing effort to make things palatable, and of a countervulgarization that renders things parched, there is being beggared out of existence a high yet workable cultural ideal, a climate in which a *sense* of art can flourish. And it seems to me that the lack of a proper climate for art is a much more serious shortcoming in America than the actual number of works of art themselves. Culture—in the old-fashioned, well-rounded sense of something civilized and civilizing alike—has not simply failed as a reality in America, but is fast fading as an ideal. Such a culture stands in relation to formal education as good wine to the grape: it is a fermentation, a mellowing, a very special and at the same time wholly characterizing element; and it permeates society in terms of its sensibilities no less than its art. One can, of course, all too easily exalt such a culture as a way of disparaging much that is essential and even healthful in modern life; and one can sigh for it on a sentimental basis, in standpat terms. All the same, any way of life that lacks its best qualities can scarcely be looked upon as cultivated at all; at any rate, no amount of education or knowledge or skill can begin to mean the same thing. And actually the climate I desiderate is no more than a salubrious, breeze-swept temperate zone; it is not forbidding, nor oppressively patrician, nor strenuously democratic. A cool, dry judgment is mingled there with gusto and generous appreciation; the people there are no more mired in the past than running wild in the present; its tone is altogether urbane without being even faintly genteel; it boasts neither untouchables nor sacred cows; it displays a constant corrective irony and perhaps not overmuch virtue; and everyone there is just sufficiently wrongheaded and prejudiced and inconsistent to be attractively human.

2

Being a curiously inartistic and ingenious people; being, also, too serious-minded to look on pleasure bare, and so commercialized as to put a price tag on Beauty, we approach art by many routes, but never by the most direct. Most frequently vulgarization sets in, the point of the story is sacrificed to the plot, Shakespeare is streamlined or Chekhov fattened up. Among the overserious there is often a process of dehydration, with only such fluid retained as has medicinal properties; or the work of art is converted from thoroughbred to packhorse and forced to stagger under a heavy sociological and psychiatric load.

Although what frankly seem to me the most delightful and rewarding qualities of art are precisely these that are slighted in many highbrow ranks today, I must admit that it is not done altogether without reason. The slighting constitutes a form of dissociation, even of protest. The sight of panders everywhere must inevitably call forth the prig; the sight of art being everywhere rouged and perfumed, groomed and tricked out for harlotry, must inspire a violent contrary wish—a wish to have art, like an orthodox Jewish bride, shorn of her locks and made as unalluring as possible. Middlebrow adulteration, its slight softening of every texture, its faint sweetening of every taste, have clearly had a hand in creating the current highbrow distrust of charms and graces. This isn't to say there need be an abundance of such qualities or that, in an age like ours, there can be. In this unquiet age, an age not even of scars but of outright wounds, clearly very little that is charming or delightful will seem central or germane. Yet though there is truth in such a statement, there is also cant. It is perhaps not necessary to dance on the edge of volcanoes; but need one ignore, or even disapprove of, the sunset because the sky may soon grow dark with bomber planes? Again, is shaving off the hair an answer to overrouging the cheeks, or a desert the corrective to a swamp? Even so, one might agree that one kind of excess tends, not unprofitably, to breed another—did not highbrow criticism, in the very act of professing to probe the tensions of contemporary life, seem so pedagogically remote from them. Art is not something marketable but neither is it something mummified; and indeed, if it is not chiefly and most palpably a form of transcendence and release, pray then what is? If the impress of style, the vivid air of distinction, the artist's ability to be uniquely expressive and intense— if these do not invite, do not indeed impose, some immediate, electrical response, can the result—however rich in cerebral or moral mineral matter—really have much to do with art itself?

I was not surprised, reading an Inquiring Reporter column on "What Is Charm?" to find a sculptor identifying charm with the prettier examples of eighteenth-century painting. It was to be assumed that charm's status would be relatively low, its character rigorously limited; that it would be equated with Sir Joshua Reynolds' children or, by extension, with Sir James M. Barrie's grownups; that it would at most signify Watteau and Fragonard, minuets and romantic ballets, Hans Andersen or Charles Lamb. No doubt the word itself has acquired vapid and even repellent connotations; and plainly writers who spray charm about without discretion are like women who mistreat an atomizer. Moreover, charm can be a strong ally of gentility and a quite conscienceless weapon of fraud: we usually do right, I think, to ask to see its credentials. But that is very far from trying to have it deported; and to suggest that, because many writers misuse charm, there is no virtue to fragrance is to come closer, I would think, to the gospel of unyielding naturalism than to any goal of truth. Ignoring such obvious charmers as Poulenc or Dufy or Walter de la Mare, if contemporary artists so unlike as Picasso, E. E. Cummings and Marianne Moore haven't, among other things, a very decided charm, what have they? Art, today, sometimes seems in danger of acquiring all the vices of science without any of the virtues. What with being anthropology's field worker and psychiatry's receptionist, art is quite prevented from cultivating its own garden.

Charm is by now too ambiguous, too merely decorative a word to be made the symbol of my own dissatisfaction. But it is clear that all the old, traditional, taken-for-granted "surface" qualities of art—distinction, fragrance, elegance, gaiety, style: those things for which we prize a Mendelssohn or a Vermeer, a Tennyson or a Congreve—such qualities, it is clear, are being slighted or ignored. No doubt *The Tempest* can be profitably viewed as something more than a masque; but to interpret it as something quite other, to regard it as principally a study in expiation, seems to me to make Shakespeare very much of an age—and an age, moreover, not his own. Possibly we are falling into the shallowness of despising the "shallow." He was the mightiest of Puritans no less than of philistines who first insisted that beauty is only skin deep. Depth, and its step-daughter Complexity, and its handmaiden Symbolism, are so much revered today, so much courted and curtsied to, as almost to obscure the fact of exactly what we mean by them, or whether—on the terms set—they aren't properly associated with philosophy rather than art. Perhaps the greatest of all our critics remarked that "poetry gives most pleasure when only generally and not perfectly understood," and he offered it as a principle to honor, not as a puzzle to resent. But so pressing now has become the critical obligation to explain or reinterpret that it is almost mandatory to pitch on something either obscure enough to need explaining or misunderstood enough by all previous critics to need to be straightened out. And since no one can burrow deep where the author happens to be shallow, we must make canyons out of molehills; we must everywhere find size and significance, those idols so much less of art than of America; and more and more our criticism suggests the tread of elephants approaching a temple.

Given our feeble artistic sense, the whole present tendency isn't too hard to grasp. Anything journalistic must be outlawed—which could be a virtue; but outlawed in terms of the pedagogical, which is almost always a vice. Everywhere people reappraise some simple classic for the small ingenious theory that isn't worth the paper that is written on it. All too frequently the creative is turned into the intellectual, soaring is replaced by delving; while art, which has always constituted the highest and noblest form of release, is more and more tinged with something so gnawing and anxious as to seem more like remorse. But surely one very great characteristic of any inherently artistic people is a sense of play—play of mind, most of all, not mere prankishness — and a natural sense of irony. The reigning current mood has quite ousted all sense of play and exhibits no working sense of irony. To be sure, irony is a much approved and discussed and dissected quality in today's approach to literature, and wherever possible, and perhaps sometimes where not, critics isolate and decipher it; but it doesn't seem very contagious.

Mr. Richard Chase, in his recent book on Emily Dickinson, deplores what he calls the rococo element in her poetry—the minor, dainty, toylike, *bibelot* aspect. And in anyone who at her best is so deeply imaginative and intense an artist as Emily Dickinson, the persistence of this merely whimsical and fanciful streak causes real injury, becomes a real misfortune. We could similarly wish that the English Metaphysicals had indulged in much fewer conceits, or that Sterne, or even Shakespeare himself—but I needn't dig for other examples. Yet where the superior artist is harmed by not rising above what we may call, with Mr. Chase, the rococo, a nation is very often harmed by not reaching up to it. The artist can dispense with the small forms of beauty, but the public cannot. The artist can function largely in a world of his own making—too much culture is perhaps even "weakening" for genius, and beautiful material objects may in a sense be the enemy of beauty. But nonartists, noncreative people, the world at large, need the atmosphere, the ornaments, the décor of culture. A predominantly *bibelot*-like culture could only, of course, be frivolous, dilettantish, effeminate. But a purely functional, no-nonsense, always-abreast-of-the-times culture, where in one's bookcase Toynbee leans only on Schweitzer and Schweitzer leans only on Freud—does this bespeak anything temperamental or personal, or is it only a part of the times? It's not a question of Old Guard and avant-garde, or whether a Canaletto print does more for a home than a Mexican primitive, or oldish things made of mahogany more than brand-new things made of metal, but whether there are not amenities and graces of the spirit; whether there are not cultures, as well as cups, that cheer. I don't contend that Jung or Margaret Mead or Frank Lloyd Wright aren't more central to our time than Osvald Siren or Sir Charles Singer; or that in order to be cultured, or well adjusted, or happy, one need be able to distinguish R. L. from G. B. Hobson, A. W. from A. F. Pollard, Oliver from André Simon, Vincent from Gertrude, or Gertrude from T. E., or T. E. from W. W., or W. W. from W. J., or W. J. from D. H. Lawrence. But for every ten educated people who have read Margaret Mead, is there one who knows which Hobson was the great authority on bindings and which on Chinese art?

Much of our own antirococoism stems, I think, from something Puritan in us. We are only given to a kind of love of the graces, a feeling for the charming in culture, when the wind is blowing from Europe; and it hasn't blown steadily from there since the 1920s. The '20s, of course, have latterly been as much romanticized as they were formerly run down. The mood of the '20s was made up of many things—not least, of that sense of promise in life, and of profusion in literature, that made us emotionally both spendthrift and carefree. But upstart and disordered and excessive though the '20s were, they were in impulse genuinely antibourgeois, antipuritan, antipedagogical: they reacted to the creative, they relished the creative, they aspired passionately to create. We lacked, then, the measure and control, the ability to select, delete, hew to the line, that constitute an artistic people; but we had, at any rate, the capacity to absorb and participate, to feel release and indulge in appreciation. We lacked the discipline, but we had the positive qualities that needed disciplining. The mood of the '20s had to pass, Depression or not; while, granted the Depression, the mood of the '30s had to be what it was. But the enduring significance of the '30s is less the purpose and propaganda that writers put into their work than the high spirits they took out of it. For the propaganda has been long discredited, but the joyousness has never been restored.

The present age is in the strong grip of cultural authoritarianism and of the most dogmatic kind. For great natural cultural lawgivers of Dr. Johnson's type there is much to be said, though even here "there is much to be said on both sides." And of course today there are not only all those who would legislate and lead, there are all the many more who hunger to be led, who crave to cry "Master." Lionel Trilling has rather chided E. M. Forster—in an age so generally contrariwise—for his "refusal to be great." One knows what Mr. Trilling means, one knows what is valid in what he means—whether with Forster specifically or with intellectuals and artists in general. A "refusal to be great" can mask a certain evasion of moral responsibility, of final decisions and allegiances. It can reflect too a certain self-consciousness, on the refuser's part, that is mere vanity; it can constitute a special, perhaps quite extreme, form of egoism. And Forster himself seems at times not merely casual but playful and frivolous. All the same, whatever personal shortcomings or debatable human traits may lodge with this attitude, it yet seems the backbone of a very notable, a very much honored, tradition—of that indeed very great tradition of skeptical humanism. It is a tradition that having said *Thus I think* next always asks *What do I know?*, a tradition that forces the very bringer of light to assay the light he brings as sharply as the darkness he dispels. In the history of thought and culture the dark nights have perhaps in some ways cost mankind less grief than the false dawns, the prison houses in which hope persists less grief than the Promised Lands where hope expires. Skeptical humanism is no enemy of positive values or even of resolute action; but men bred to that tradition will continue to feel that their values must be exhibited, warts and all, and must in the end be made to speak for themselves. About any other method, including the acceptance of greatness, there is always at least a touch of *force majeure* and perhaps even a drop or two of patent medicine. Today anyone's refusal to be great seems the more formulated for being so out of line with prevailing thought. The Great Men, the Strong Men, of literature today are men of fierce passions and strong convictions, men playing the role of prophet, teacher, moralist, martyr, saint, sinner, seer—the Melvilles, Nietzsches, Kierkegaards, the Gides, Dostoevskys, D. H. Lawrences. Some of these men are as individual, one or two are now and then as skeptical, as Forster; but the real point is to what degree have they encouraged independence, individualism, skepticism, the relaxed will, in others?

If only because the tide has been running strong against the old humanist attitude, the Forsters with their relaxed wills and their refusals to be great must take on a special value. The tradition of Socrates, of Montaigne and Erasmus, of Hume and of the Enlightenment, all the more because it never flourishes *below* the cultured classes, is immensely vital to them, is what we might almost call their claim to culture. It seems to me an absolutely essential tradition for societies and nations in need of something equable as well as affirmative, in need of lasting daylight as well as glowing dawns. It is a tradition that has never really established itself in America—a corollary, I think, to our being an inartistic people; it is a tradition, at any rate, at variance with a people who love the *idea* of greatness, who love panaceas, and formulas, and solutions, and absolutions, and reassuring answers. To a nation that worships God and Mammon both there must be something profoundly uncongenial in an attitude that blindly worships nothing. From the failure of the humanist tradition to participate fully or to act decisively, civilization may perhaps crumble or perish at the hands of barbarians. But unless the humanist tradition itself in some form survives, there can really be no civilization at all.

2. The Broadway Blues

RATHER than do any circuit tour of the arts in America, most of which I'm not qualified to discuss, I would take a look—cultural rather than critical—at the theater. I have spent sixteen years reviewing plays, which means that during the season I have averaged two or three nights a week in the theater, and which means, too, that I have been part of a particular, highly professional first night audience. But the theater seems to me a sound choice for more than my happening to be familiar with it. For one thing, it is an extremely public and an extremely much publicized medium, whose activities—backstage almost as much as on stage—are constantly on display. Beyond that it is—in the commercial sense—a highly concentrated medium: New York is as decidedly the seat of show business as is Washington of government. The theater is in some sense, too, a "class" art; it stands pricewise quite apart from such mass media as radio, television and the movies. And the theater, finally, is an *established* art, one with world-wide and centuries-old traditions—not something as new as television or as "American" as the movies; an art that, not being American itself, must reveal, in its Broadway form, how much of an American impress it has acquired.

The theater preens itself as the queen of public entertainments, the ranking debutante or reigning dowager over cinema, cinerama, radio, television, basketball, the circus, penny arcades, horse shows, street parades and political rallies: as for ballet and opera, it quickly disposes of them as not entertainments at all.* The queen of entertainments it

* It is, I think, literally true that more than half the people in the theater could not, before *South Pacific*, have told you who Ezio Pinza was.

38

may or may not be, but in America it is very plainly the scullion of the arts. The movies and TV are much more obvious easy marks; they are far more vividly American; their blunders, their timidities, their vulgarities make far sprightlier copy. But their only real better claim to be Horrible Examples is their wider application: the theater offers equal proof of our artistic shortcomings at a good deal more shameful level. For better or worse, the movies and TV are overwhelmingly mass-production commodities, Big Business operations.

When Mr. Robert Sherwood signed a contract to write plays for TV, presumably his great triumph consisted in his being able to deal directly with top officials rather than—as in Hollywood—being subject to hierarchic humiliations. But if the Hollywood system is as professionally misguided as it is culturally appalling, it yet conforms to the standard big-business pattern. Moreover, the movies and TV are affected by all our national shibboleths, hayseed tastes, provincial prejudices and small-town intolerances. Any final verdict on Hollywood or television must be tied in with a comprehensive evaluation of American society. The Broadway theater, whatever its own difficulties, is bothered by no such problems. Yet despite the fact that—owing to movies, radio and TV—the theater has most lost ground as a *popular* medium, it has become more of a popular medium than ever. Despite being, on a price basis, a class medium, it has culturally grown more and more *déclassé*. Wherever it is not an outright plebeian circus, it tends to be a merely more "sophisticated" bourgeois playground.

Let us be as fair, and also as sensible, about the theater as we can. Its world is a very special one. Even as a form of art, it thrives peculiarly on effect; as a commercial institution, it depends immensely on display. Something that draws for its final and composite effect upon so many sources—poetry, painting, music, dance, pantomime, singing, declamation—can't easily avoid being impure and exploitative, nor adulterating where it means to blend. Something that draws for its final and composite effect upon so many talents—author, actor, director, composer, designer, choreographer—can't help altering, amplifying, distorting—and generally compromising. And people who are holding the mirror up to nature can only be expected, and at not too wide intervals, to keep glancing into it themselves.

Toward all the gush, bravura and nonsense of the performers, toward the whole greenroom side of the theater, one is naturally indulgent: temperament, like liberty, is important despite how many crimes are committed in its name. As a business, too, the theater is very special. With rare exceptions the producer has to work with other people's money and in actual practice is often as much peddler as impresario. The theater isn't just a sensible business. Actors don't get enough work; producers don't have enough capital; backers accept very poor odds against a highly problematical return.* In most cases the theater, so far from being a sound business risk, is the merest gamble. Yet the weird thing about it is that this most unbusinesslike of professions displays the most consistently commercial aims.

That, businesslike or not, the aims should be largely commercial, the types of entertainment largely popular, is quite understandable. One may personally deplore the level of even the most avowedly popular entertainment; one may wonder whether the formulas need be so childish or the gags so brassy—whether, whatever its IQ or its theater tastes, an average audience wouldn't respond to something a little fresher and more individual. In view of the immense popularity of, say, a *Voice of the Turtle* or an *Oklahoma!,* might not such shows, on Broadway at least, be considered a popular norm rather than quality stuff that happened to click? But all this is really incidental, for the out-and-out commercial production at least has no split personality, at least makes no phony pretenses; it is strictly business, and its miscalculations are exactly those of a dress designer or an automobile manufacturer.

It is true that only a trifling amount of such determinedly popular stuff proves successful, so that *on its own terms* the commercial theater is by and large an ignominious and thoroughly ludicrous failure: popular theater entertain-

---

* Perhaps one play in six or seven is a hit, and backers cut into the profits not on a dollar-for-dollar basis but on a 50c-on-the-dollar one. Moreover, many hits bring neither backers nor producers a cent. *Show Boat,* when revived, played to packed houses for a solid year yet never earned back its original investment.

ment must be condemned as bad business without even asking whether it is bad amusement or art. If it is a melancholy fact that some 80 per cent of theater producers are no more than junk dealers, it is a comic fact that they cannot make junk pay. They will tell you that it costs too much to produce and operate. They will look bewildered if you tell them that, for the average couple, the run of their junk costs a great deal too much to see. For a show that the average couple finds pleasant enough, but no more so than any number of B movies, the price for two seats may be $9.60. The location of the two seats may well be the sixteenth row far over to the side; moreover, the seats may have had to be bought nine weeks in advance and to be sat in on a night when New York is having a blizzard. The producer refuses to face the fact that for—at most—$3.00 the same couple could go to an equally pleasant movie on any night it chooses, sit in better seats and have newsreels, shorts and probably a stage show thrown in. The producer, in other words, refuses to weigh the fact that, simply as popular entertainment, the theater faces terrific competition. Broadway is in very much the same situation as the railroads—it is menaced by movies, radio and television as are the railroads by trucks, busses, planes and cars—and it has done even less, if possible, than the railroads to win itself friends. Most producers, when they have a big hit, snap their fingers at the public: in their heart of hearts they really think that the public exists to come to the aid of their flops.

But the real failure of the theater, the real evidence of its prevailing shallowness, its lack of standards, of convictions, of courage (and of course the lack of convictions helps account for the lack of courage), has to do with what functions, not as a mass but as a class medium. The true, deep failure emerges when one has got past the anonymous faces in the audience at a run-of-the-mine opening night, when one has got past the irrelevant name of the playwright, the unfamiliar names of the backers. The true, deep failure emerges on the most high-toned of opening nights, on the Social Register and Café Society personalities in the audience; on the Dun-and-Bradstreet names of the backers; on the immensely relevant name of the playwright, and the producer, and the director, and the star. Here what passes for good taste, what preens itself as sophistication, is not only graciously pleased to be represented but couldn't be paid to stay away.

Tonight's opening, let us imagine, is a light, smart comedy—a comedy worth study, since what the upper middle class laughs at is perhaps more significant than what it ponders or weeps over. As for the author, a pet playwright of the rich, like a pet dressmaker or caterer or jeweler, must know—must indeed know above everything else—how to please; he must know by instinct what to tone down or leave out, what will bore or antagonize the audience or rub it the wrong way. There is of course the chance—particularly if the author isn't an old hand at such plays—that he had very little to do with it all. All too aware that the theater is a co-operative enterprise, Broadway has long drawn the inference that it is the playwright who must co-operate. Brought up on the chestnut that plays are not written but rewritten, Broadway instinctively feels that any completed script, no matter how polished or pleasing, is best treated as a rough draft. Once when I wrote a play and a star expressed a great wish to appear in it if I'd sort of turn it into something else, one of my producers, who saw nothing untoward in the request, rebuked me with: "Why, you've only rewritten your play once: almost nothing of ours gets on till it's been rewritten five or six times." Though such comment didn't appreciably help me as a playwright, I found it vastly illuminating as a reviewer. It helped explain that form of double dismay that overtakes one, time and again, at so-called better-quality productions: the sense, on the one hand, of an endless cutting down and compromising with standards and, on the other hand, of bleaching out all the personal color the play once had by giving it a whole succession of washings. And this is often as commercially misguided as it is artistically depraved. What producers refuse (even on a commercial basis) to see is that in any play that shows talent and individuality a 20-per-cent gain in slickness and smoothness usually means a 50-per-cent loss of freshness or urgency in the original script. There is really nothing worse than a glaring mixture of the hand-made and the machine-made, the spontaneous and the slick—if only because each does nothing to point up the virtues, and everything to emphasize the weaknesses, of the other.

The "quality" theater is most insistent of all on the need for varnish, whether on rotting timber or good sound natural wood. Those who dominate the quality theater worship appearances behind the footlights to exactly the same degree that they do everywhere else. This isn't for a moment to disparage varnish. Plainly, moreover, anything involving so many people as a theatrical production can't help creating disorder: kinks will have to be ironed out, and a certain amount of glossing over will prove a virtue if only because it proves a necessity. Play-production is a very confusing operation, and any playwright who isn't an utter egomaniac about his work, or a fanatical intransigent in his principles, must often become most confused of all. A play that didn't require changes or couldn't profit from suggestions would be a very remarkable one.* But the trouble lies elsewhere. Of changes made in production—in so-called superior plays—far more seem to be made in terms of the investment than of the play itself. The point is not whether the disputed line seems funny, but whether the audience—often some strange hit-or-miss tryout audience—will laugh. It is not whether a scene is psychologically or dramatically sound, but whether the audience will swallow it. It is not whether the play has the right ending, but whether the ticket holders will go home in the "right" mood. Most sadly of all, it is because plays, up to the very last moment, are susceptible of change that they are subject to change: their fluidity, which, if not abused, could be a powerful advantage, is today so shamelessly exploited as to constitute the Broadway stage's most consistent form of harlotry. The out-of-town tryout, which presumably exists to give the production all possible grace and polish, has become a mere gimmick for making people pay at the box office while the show is undergoing repairs on the stage. A *Variety* review of an out-of-town opening—unlike a *Retail Bookseller* review of a forthcoming book—is not

---

* Which is not to argue that the playwright should—or creatively even *could*—make the changes.

simply regarded as a professional appraisal of box-office chances. It is often a signal—and guide—to rewrite, and most often, moreover, in the case of quality productions. The stories (whether told humorously in the flush of subsequent success, or bitterly in the aftermath of failure) of plays that were better in Boston than on Broadway, of pressures put upon an already worn-down and worn-out playwright, of ultimatums delivered by producers and directors, of last-minute rewrite jobs in a foreign hand—these stories reveal a great many things, but more than any one thing else a capacity to be brutally tough in bossing the job, and yet the most contemptible jellyfish in not sticking by one's guns or having faith in one's own original judgment.

That the "investment" bulks tremendously large is understandable enough, and it is as wrong for any critic of Broadway behavior not to look high costs in the face as for Broadway to look nothing else. Yet one can, doubtless a little airily, suggest that if costs are so high, that is all the more reason for a producer to double-test his product—and his faith in it—*at the outset*. And one can also, and not too airily, raise the question whether with better plays the costs—or at any rate the initial ones—*need* be so high. The truth is that the quality production, being geared not to people of culture but to the well-heeled bourgeoisie, is as obedient to upper-middle-class tastes in décor as to their tastes in everything else. I am far from being opposed to expensive, not to say lavish, décor on principle, but it is one thing to relish it for what it is worth and another to let the tail wag the dog. The more stylish backers and producers who are the first to scream bloody murder about costs must know that it is their own kind that makes costs so high, that it is their own kind who would complain bitterly if the sets and costumes hadn't a maximum gloss and dash. (And at $4.80 or maybe $6.00 or even $7.20 a seat, one has the right to complain, exactly as at a luxury hotel that lacked luxuriousness.) The quality play is, indeed, all too often a mere luxury play: to satisfy the carriage trade, the producer must himself contrive to keep a carriage. Even the most intelligent playwrights and producers won't, when put to it, slash costs by doing without expensive décor and extensive scene shifting; it's too risky a move. The unions enter here, and they are often highhanded and by that very token shortsighted; but if painted scenery or simple backdrops became the rule, the unions would have to play along. Productions like *Don Juan in Hell,* which, with their paraphernalia reduced to a few suitcases, can not only operate on a small budget but can play one-night stands in college towns and other places with a cultivated population, point a valuable lesson. If "quality" plays were aimed as much at the professional and intellectual classes as at the carriage trade, not only would scenery come to count for much less, but serious and honest subject matter would count for much more. As it now stands, the quality play must often be as much slicked up and glossed over as the popular one.

There is also the business of the critics. This being a cultural rather than critical analysis of the theater, I can pass over much that, from a different standpoint, is controversial. The *cultural* facts, it seems to me, are pretty simple. No one would deny that some sort of reviewing of plays is necessary, or at any rate better than no sort. The critics' competence and the critics' standards are matters of real cultural importance; but it is overwhelmingly true that the daily-paper critics, who almost always decide the fate of plays, have never seemed so fanatically on the side of culture as to damn the commercial play out of hand. The nub is never their competence or standards, anyhow: only their power. And high production costs have greatly increased their power. If critics pan a show, it costs too much to keep it going until the producer can have appealed from the critics to the public. This is an unhappy state of affairs, but it would scarcely be happier were critics —as producers all but suggest—to go easy on plays. For one thing, the ruinous finances of show business have changed the whole problem of reviewing from the realistic to the almost comic: with most plays today it's not only fatal if the critics write bad reviews; it's almost as fatal if they don't write the next thing to raves. "Mixed," or so-so, or favorable but not "selling" notices make producers almost as glum (and indignant) as straight-out pans.* The reason, in the prevailing jargon, is that any play that's not a hit today is a flop. That a play might run, say, for three months—which, translated into book sales, would mean at least 50,000 copies—counts for nothing. The truth is that no play satisfies its producer unless it does enormously better *on Manhattan Island* than a terrifically best-selling book does throughout the entire United States. Naturally, what the critics say is important. But does the producer ever try to minimize this importance, to play *down* the critics' role? Indeed not: for all their screaming, producers do everything possible to play it up, to increase the critics' power—taking large display ads full of quotes and even on occasion large skysigns.

And if the critics have far too much power, the so-called quality theater certainly gives them every chance to use it "adversely." For the whole prevailing tone† of Broadway's "superior" offerings is insistently slick, showy, philistine, adulterate, catch-as-catch-can, is as fundamentally indifferent to *real* quality, to true art, as it is lacking in all respect toward it. This is meant here not as critical condemnation but simply as cultural analysis: what follows, in other words, isn't meant to show what's wrong with the theater in terms of its plays, but rather what's wrong with America in terms of its theater. We must look at Broadway where Broadway most preens and publicizes itself, at the people and things it is proudest and most admiring of. Thus the best known and most admired backer of plays is Mr. Howard Cullman. Every season there are newspaper and magazine articles concerning how he and Mrs. Cullman choose the plays they invest in; every season the plays they invest in are sufficient news to become matters of public record. From time to time there is a respectful list-

---

* One of the most serious writers for the theater once severely lectured me for not putting my praise in the first paragraph and my strongest praise in the first sentence. The theory is that most readers glance at the beginning of a review and the end, and that as a result reviewers should gear their notices to this widespread habit. Owing, I suppose, to the importance of the daily-paper reviews, serious playwrights no less than business-minded producers take a completely commercial attitude toward the reviews they get. They don't, whatever they may say, primarily want reviews that show understanding of their plays or that would commend their play to intelligent theatergoers; they want reviews that will sell a great many tickets, which can only mean a great many tickets to utter nitwits.

† There are, of course—here as elsewhere—very real exceptions; but they have, very decidedly, the status of exceptions.

ing of the Cullman successes, a humorous reference to their financial mistakes. The lists range from a fair number of box-office plays, through perhaps an equal number of better plays with a box-office angle, to a smallish number of "quality" plays and name revivals. The whole operation is conducted as a business, with the implied joker that show business itself is not one, that there is a considerable horse-racing element involved, with the Cullmans themselves having the fun of being handicappers.

All this is completely unexceptionable; the Cullmans not only have every right to their hobby but in their own way are genuinely devoted to the theater. It is not what they do that raises any kind of question; it is only what they don't do. What they don't do is to assume that traditional and responsible role assumed in relation to the arts by rich people from Maecenas to Otto Kahn: they seem to prefer making money they don't need to giving *art* the assistance it does. And their names carry just that sort of cachet: the implications, for any play the Cullmans are known to have invested in, are much less that it is a good play than that it is a good gamble.

If Mr. Cullman's is the greatest success story among backers, Mr. Joshua Logan's is challenged only by Rodgers and Hammerstein as the greatest Broadway success story of all. And it is no less symbolic and symptomatic than it is great: Mr. Logan is *par excellence* a man of the theater—producer, director, adapter, coauthor—so that his fabulous success touches almost every facet of the contemporary theater itself. Mr. Logan directed such hits as *John Loves Mary*, *The Happy Time*, *South Pacific*, *Picnic*. He coauthored as well as directed *Mister Roberts* and *Wish You Were Here*. In *The Wisteria Trees* he gave a Deep-South American setting, and his own slant, to Chekhov's *The Cherry Orchard*. In terms of box office and popular esteem, his contribution has been tremendous. To straight box-office plays, to such things as *John Loves Mary* and *The Happy Time*, he has consistently brought a skill and savvy that have pointed up any good qualities in the script. To a work like *South Pacific* (which, quite irrelevantly, I didn't much care for), that without him would probably have been a very sentimental and soupy affair, Mr. Logan brought a certain needed briskness and bounce; he made it, as it were, the blooming offspring of *Mister Roberts* and *Madame Butterfly*. And to *Mister Roberts* itself he gave a frequent stage zip and farcical high spirits.

Given anything whose values and virtues are of the surface, or merely of the theater, Mr. Logan will skillfully exploit and almost always enhance his materials. But so soon as he starts working in more genuinely human, or complex, or delicate material; so soon as a scene or a character or even a speech seeks to be *expressive* rather than merely effective, or to have true intensity rather than mere punch, Mr. Logan seems not merely at sea but actually at odds with his material. He has, superlatively, the theater mind without the artist's sensibility; one might say, too, that he has a kind of genius for contriving an effect—without grasping the effect (from another point of view) of what he has done. What was engaging about Arthur Kober's *Having a Wonderful Time* was a certain warmth and humanity; it was precisely those things, in the musical comedy Mr. Logan and Mr. Kober made from it, that were lacking. What seemed real about William Inge's *Picnic* was a certain sense of the lostness and blind mischance of life; but as projected by Mr. Logan on a stage, the play had a neon-lighted theatricality that achieved the wrong kind of effect at the cost of the right kind of appeal. But the best indication of Mr. Logan's theater mind is what he did with *The Cherry Orchard*—in small effect after small effect—but most crucially in the final scene of the play—in, as it happens, the most celebrated curtain the theater boasts since Nora slammed the door behind her. No longer, while the sound of the axes is heard, is the old servant left behind in the locked-up deserted house; in *The Wisteria Trees* he has most humanely and carefully been removed to a hospital. There was a story—which may be no more than a story—that the original ending of *The Wisteria Trees* had followed Chekhov but that during the pre-Broadway tryout out-of-town audiences were aghast that anyone so charming as Helen Hayes would be heartless enough to lock her old servant up in a deserted house and that he was accordingly transferred to a hospital. If the story is true, it points up a really immense misconception; for perhaps nowhere else in literature have we so perfect an example of thoughtlessness, *rather than heartlessness,* of people who are irresponsible rather than callous. But whatever Mr. Logan's reason for discarding Chekhov's ending, it was the last and deepest stroke of his own ax upon *The Cherry Orchard.*

My reason for bringing in Mr. Logan here is not a critical but a purely cultural one; is concerned not with Mr. Logan himself, but with his enormous prestige in the Broadway, which is to say the American, theater. It is a prestige largely derived from his huge box-office successes; a salute to his being a very great *practical* man of the theater.

Mr. Oscar Hammerstein, who forms with Richard Rodgers the most successful and celebrated of living theater teams, is another, but a rather different, case in point. As the librettist of *Oklahoma!, Carousel, Allegro, South Pacific, The King and I* and *Me and Juliet,* Mr. Hammerstein —whether inventing or, much oftener, adapting his material—has set the tone for the Rodgers & Hammerstein musicals. Though superficially the musicals are not alike (indeed, Rodgers and Hammerstein try very hard not to repeat their successes), they have certain traits in common, as well as traits that are—or were—uncommon in musicals generally. They tell human, often rather pathetic, stories; they strike, for musical comedy, a rather earnest note and are treated, as musicals go, in rather earnest fashion. In Hammerstein librettos important characters die, or they go through moral crises involving right and wrong values. Compared to the generally frivolous tone of musicals, and indeed to the satiric tone of Rodgers' earlier work with Lorenz Hart, the Rodgers & Hammerstein shows suggest a mildly liberalistic musical Era of Good Feeling.

And just this, in conjunction with Mr. Hammerstein's gifts as a librettist, sets his musicals apart from most others, in a cultural as well as a theatrical sense. Yet, after allowing that Mr. Hammerstein—to use one of Broadway's favorite words—is one of Broadway's most literate librettists, one must look twice even at what makes him distinctive. Thus the handsome quota of moral virtue in his librettos seems most of the time a decided theatrical vice. Too often the librettos simply fail to be gay without ever be-

coming properly serious; they swim in a sea of facile sentiment, glib idealism and humanitarian clichés. The matter
is really a simple one: Mr. Hammerstein has raised the
libretto a notch or two above its traditionally ghastly level,
has brought it to about the level of women's magazine fiction
or B movies. Instead of being an insult to the middle-brow
intelligence, he has made the libretto a sop to the middlebrow emotions. Mr. Hammerstein would never have made
Mr. Logan's mistake of taking the humanity of *Having a
Wonderful Time;* he is full of human feeling, feeling that
very often is of an exact piece with his audience's; he is
superior to his audience in articulateness, not in insight.

Mr. Hammerstein's superiority is, in the actual Broadway scheme of things, a real one: it represents the second-
rate in relation to the third-rate.* And what is culturally
most deceptive and most consoling in the American theater
—indeed in all the arts in America—is the second-rate
rather than the third. For it's not only that the third-rate
is so mechanical, meretricious and shallow as to stand self-
exposed; it's that the second-rate is very gratefully regarded as a *corrective*. And in that sense it impedes progress at least as much as it represents it. To put it very
simply: Mr. Hammerstein isn't good *enough;* and since one
of his fervent beliefs is that the audience is always right,
he will probably never be any better. The idea that a play
which fails commercially can yet be an artistic success he
has curtly dismissed as "bosh."† If Mr. Hammerstein
wished to say that it is financially dangerous, and even
ruinous, to appeal to minority tastes, he would have a
valid practical point; but to flatter the public with such a
philistine rule of thumb, to characterize all art as simply
synonymous with box office, is quite something else. Mr.
Hammerstein himself, moreover, must know that very often

* In the case of Rodgers and Hammerstein, the situation is complicated by the
fact that Mr. Rodgers *is* a first-rate composer of show music. But despite much
excellent Rodgers music in Rodgers & Hammerstein musicals, there has also crept
in the kind of thing that would never have done so in any collaboration with Lorenz
Hart. Had Mr. Rodgers done a "Bali Ha'i" in his Rodgers & Hart days, it would
have clearly been done as a travesty; and Mr. Hart would never have provided
opportunities for such inflated musical utterance as Mr. Hammerstein almost made
mandatory in *Allegro*.

† Mr. Hammerstein has also asserted that it is a playwright's obligation to be
understood by a large number of people, not by a "negligible few." But are, say,
40,000 people in a single city a "negligible few"? Because 40,000 ticket buyers
will still leave most productions sadly in the red.

the *play* isn't even the decisive element; that a play which could fail without, let us say, the Lunts can succeed handsomely with them; that, reasoning as Mr. Hammerstein does, even *Hamlet* can only become an "artistic success" with the assistance of a Maurice Evans.

My object with Mr. Cullman, Mr. Logan and Mr. Hammerstein is to document the fact that they are not simply products but partisans of a commercial theater and a box-office culture. I say this not for moral protest but for factual analysis. There are noncommercial playwrights on Broadway, even a few flourishing ones, and there are many theater people who, given the chance, would, I think, pursue largely noncommercial aims. But in general Broadway is deficient both in the more discriminative kind of backing and in taste and talent. Of the two, we must decidedly have the right kind of backing first, for until we get it on a solid and permanent basis the right kind of taste and talent must, in large measure, become either muffled or alienated. Until we possess, along with a commercial theater, a straightforwardly noncommercial one (which needn't be uncommercial); until we develop a stage that isn't subject to pressures, isn't marred by caprices, isn't in constant panic that if *this* production flops there will be no others, the theater cannot have any true cultural or artistic identity. The financial need is thus for *support of the theater,* not for the backing of individual plays— exactly as, in other arts, the financial need is for maintaining a symphony orchestra or art museum, not for performing particular compositions or exhibiting particular paintings. And however sad it may be that there are no sustaining patrons of the drama, as there are of art and music, the fault is perhaps the theater's own. Where opera, symphony orchestras and art museums frankly ask for money because they need it, and think that their aim justifies the asking for it, "serious" theater people somehow always introduce a gimmick, always bring in the commercial angle along with the cultural one, always imply that their play may be a winner, are always willing to package a play that *is* art along with one that isn't. As a result, the possible patron is approached on an ambiguous, contradictory basis: the whole project isn't good enough to invest in for profit nor pure enough to support as a cause. As things now stand, no one can be blamed for refusing to become a patron of the theater while consenting, at the same time, to become a patron of something else. But a truly noncommercial theater, on a sustained and long-term basis, is the only real solution; and not for art's sake only, but so that we can also render unto Broadway the things—the often perfectly sound and attractive things—that are Broadway's.

3. TV: A Prospectus

Two phenomena—a half century apart— have exercised the greatest influence on twentieth-century Americans as social animals. The first was the arrival of the automobile which—aside from its more practical uses—stimulated all America to move about, whether five miles to a picture show, twenty-five to a bathing beach, fifty for the sake of driving or two hundred to call on Grandma. With the coming of the automobile there took place, in the strictest sense, a social revolution. Distance, previously a barrier, was now an incentive; the rare treat became the everyday occurrence; in alliance with the telephone, the automobile could whisk you from the fireside to the ten-mile-distant poker table, from the side-yard swing to the mountains. It was no longer necessary to eat at home, and hence to keep servants, or even to sleep at home or, with the coming of the trailer, even to have a home. One could savor life to a degree never before imagined, and on as free-moving and last-minute a basis as one chose. The whole method of courtship (for buggy riding had been largely rural) was altered, and, scarcely less, the whole enjoyment of sex. The suburbs lost their remoteness; while what had been a day's grudged and dutiful pilgrimage —to visit the sick, the old, the poor, the near-of-kin—could be effected in two or three hours; and where, on a rainy, a snowy or even a chilly night, the half-mile walk to the car line had kept hundreds of thousands at home, they need now only stroll to the garage. While forfeiting nothing as a refuge, home became much less of a prison; and even those accustomed to live snug, in the bliss of carpet slippers, book and reading lamp, relished the chance of living strenuously.

But now, a few decades after the automobile sent all
America forth upon the highroad, television has appeared
to keep all America at home. More and more the typical
American, known to all the world as an irresistible force,
is becoming an immovable object. More and more, whatever siren voices beckon from afar, the TV set, like a good
wife, holds one at its side. And more and more TV has
more and more to offer. Everyone by now has seen Shelley
— or Eisenhower or Winston Churchill — plain, and any
moment will see them in color. Every type of news event—
coronations and inaugurations, war and UN, strikes and
Un-American committees; every style, again, of entertainment — plays and movies, operas and ball games, prize
fights and tennis tournaments; every quiz rich in largess,
every comedian rife with gags—but this inventory of TV
is beginning to sound like a testimonial. All I meant was
that the highroad, from henceforth, must fight a losing
battle against the home.

Unhappily, however, television cannot be said to have
re-established home life: far more, indeed, than the automobile, it is tending to destroy it. Where Mother and
Father, Jane and John, on their treks and travels exchanged
pleasantries and ideas, they sit now for hours, side by side,
often shoulder to shoulder, scarcely exchanging a glance.
Or if they do address one another, they do so crossly, cam-
paigning for this program or that. And where friends and
families once gathered with high-minded aims—to over-
eat and then settle back and snooze; to gossip briskly, to
the ruin of a few good reputations; to glare at one another
across the bridge table, or hear an eight-year-old recite—
now, having driven some twenty miles, one is admitted
without greeting and squeezed and shushed into place.
There may, though again there may not, be an interval for
dining; but had there never been a fourth Earl of Sandwich,
television would have found it necessary to invent him.

The sad part of all this is not how much one exaggerates
but how little.* It would be inaccurate to contend that
television has ousted all other pleasures. Gambling still

---

* Leonard Lyons recorded a yarn of a father who found his small son sitting in
front of a TV set clutching a small suitcase. "He's running away from home,"
explained the boy's mother, "as soon as the program's over."

flourishes, and the theater goes grumbling on; and baseball and football remain, though watching them on the spot is largely passé. Where a book, for millions of Americans, served as a last resort, a magazine as the merest time killer and the radio as something to turn on but not necessarily to listen to, television now solaces almost any social disappointment, now supersedes almost any social activity.

We can't yet accurately determine how far-reaching, how all-encompassing, how dehumanizing the effect of television may be—for one thing because a race accustomed to it since infancy hasn't yet matured, for another because television is merely in its infancy itself. A dozen years hence it may have a hundred times its present ability to enthrall and enchain. Yet it has already come far. Never in history has there existed such an all-purpose toy for people of all ages; it has already virtually destroyed the need for newspapers, picture papers, magazines, books, plays, movies, newsreels, sports, gossip columns, speechmaking; already it takes us into courtrooms and operating rooms, churches and senates; it has begun to replace the schoolroom and in time will compete with the seminar (so that a man who is wholly illiterate can be genuinely learned). Soon enough we shall be a race of shut-ins; and the poor miserable "thrust-out"—the pauper or crank who, for lack of a TV set, must venture forth after man or woman or God—will be a most anomalous object. Already the watchword of households throughout the land is "Why go out?" Very soon, in families that can afford a cook—and her own TV set to console her for her cooking—it may be "Why get up?" Where else could one be so gregarious as among all the people on TV; where else could life prove so colorful and broadening and varied?

When the joking has been put aside and the prejudices allowed for, the whole problem of TV needs very sober analysis. One can hedge by repeating the obvious—that soundly produced and discreetly consumed, television can have immense value, can with equal vividness inform, instruct and amuse. One can repeat the no less obvious—that at small cost, in millions of homes, it can brighten, broaden, freshen existence. Clearly—if TV achieved the level of the BBC's Third Program—it could prove a source of great pleasure and value to all educated Americans. But the Third Program functions not only on a definite quality basis but—what is quite as important—on a definite quantity one. Quite as much as it isn't everyday stuff, it's not all-day stuff. Moreover, the Third Program is radio, not television.

But in all it is and seemingly ever hopes to be, television is simply a menace to America's cultural and social life. It is a menace just because there it sits, a constant temptation, gratification, time killer, solace: you have it, why not use it? your book's a wee bit boring, why not shut it and turn on TV? It is an additional menace, of course, for being commercially sponsored, and so not only riddled with the imbecilities of announcers but splotched with the timidities of sponsors. But it is perhaps most a menace in the sense that the better it is the worse it must be; that the more skill it exhibits, the more big news it conveys, the more big names it can boast, the more druglike must be its hold on vast numbers of people. Thus far it has liberated a lot of potential victims simply from proving too dull, clumsy or trite to hold them. But once it has at every level something sure-fire to purvey, once the gags have lost their brashness and the commercials cease to jar, what competing inducement will have a chance of winning out? Think what a TV set does for the man who owns one. It poses no great economic problem, for it costs little to operate and can eventually be traded in. The owner has no transportation problem—at the most, a walk down the hall or up the stairs. He no longer has an entertainment problem—here is amusement, and to spare; or an information problem—here is something more up-to-the-minute than any newspaper. As for the cultural problem, TV promises to offer everything known in plays, operas, concerts and ballets, and to dramatize the contents of all sorts of books. In time it will certainly find ways—ways no quiz show yet has dreamed of—to satisfy its audiences' gambling instincts. I don't know that it can lick the problem of sex, though with time it may simply extinguish the desire for any.

There is, of course, the question of a saturation point. Doubtless even the worst addicts will want a night off. But popular tastes being what they are, it is hard to see how an instrument with such varied charms, that keeps so abreast of the times, can possibly lose out. TV may, like telephones or cars, come to be taken for granted, but it is hard to conceive of anything that will put it on the shelf. Doubtless it merely replaces *in concentrated form* a whole cluster of previous interests. But actually it doesn't just replace them. It increases the amount and guarantees the continuity of entertainment—and without making you open your pocketbook, put on your shoes or crane your neck. And it quite does away with the tiresome "human" element, the need at times for forced conversation. On the whole, it is true, conversation in middle-class America is not only a lost art but a discarded habit. Except highball or soup spoon in hand, relatively few Americans like to have extended conversation at all; they much prefer cards, parlor games, movies, sports. Nevertheless, till the advent of TV there was a good deal of enforced or makeshift or at least intermittent conversation. People, at times, were foiled of a "fourth," or waiting for one to arrive; tennis courts were sometimes wet, or afternoons were rainy. But now, with their hand on the highball, they can turn their eyes on the screen. And there is not only far less conversation when people come together; there is far less coming together. TV is a blow to social life, however inadequate social life may generally have been. And TV is equally a blow to the life of the self; it is now the camera eye, and not the inward one, that is the bliss of solitude.

Far more significant, far more sinister than the specific dreariness of the programs or objectionableness of the commercials are, as I have hinted, the consequences of TV's merely existing. A new race seems destined to arise, with a wholly new feeling about social relations, about the need for companions or the nature of friendship. Courtship—for a new reason—will consist almost entirely of handholding. And people, as time goes on, will communicate less and less with themselves. There is thus the real problem, among millions of Americans, of ossified inner resources, of atrophied social responses. The whole tenor of the machine age has been toward just this drying up within, this deadening, flattening, standardizing without. In an automobile civilization, which was one of constant motion and activity, there was almost no time to think; in a television one, there is small desire. (TV, it must be very seriously said, is no mere gadget; it is one of the great milestones and possibly gravestones in the whole history of culture.)

One further question does crop up: Won't the triumph of TV, the shift from being not enough at home to being too much, sharply reduce the pace of American living? Finding escape in their own back yard, amusement in their own front room, may not men develop a *Ruhfleisch* they had altogether lost? May not their lives shed the old frantic hurry, the old feverish rush? Most particularly, may not those who had farthest to go for their pleasures— people in the suburbs and the country—now feel small impulse to move at all? I suspect there may be a real change in pace, a real difference in living. Not only will people remain home of nights; they will also genuinely relax. Above all, TV—while allowing actual rest—will alleviate an existing restlessness, will keep people perfectly content who, after dinner, hanker for a bridge game or a movie, a drive somewhere or a drink. Whatever the fate of the mind, the body should be saved a great deal of wear and tear.

There may thus come about a real shift in social exist-ence, from an all-too-active state to an all-too-passive one, from the benzedrine of being on the go to the bromide of sticking to the chair. From being mindlessly in motion, huge numbers of Americans may sit mindlessly motionless. I am speaking, of course, of leisure hours, of after-business habits. Whether such after-business habits will have any effect on business itself is exceedingly doubtful. It may well be that with the greater assurance of folding one's legs for the evening after reaching home the average American will only move faster than ever and farther than ever by day, that daytime activity will madly accelerate. The very basis of television's triumph may even, eventu-ally, bring about its defeat. From having stayed home of nights to enjoy television, men grown more active by day may come home of nights completely exhausted; and all over the land the ablest of newscasters, the lithest of athletes, the gayest of entertainers may perform for people sprawled out snoring in their chairs.

4. Microscopes and Telescopes

Microscopes and telescopes actually disturb a man's sense of sight. —GOETHE

IT is one of the more astringent joys of the age that never was knowledge so deeply respected nor ignorance—at certain levels—so wonderfully rife. We have enthroned the expert, at the cost not just of unseating the man of enlightenment but of paying the expert staggering sums with the chance of being misinformed. And even where he can be relied upon in his special field, he is apt to be grossly uninformed outside it; while the run-of-the-mine commentator can be almost indecently ignorant. Thus, a theater columnist isn't content to say that a musical comedy is to be made from Puccini's *Aida;* he adds that the project is inspired by the successful adapting of Puccini's *Carmen.* The theater, to be sure, boasts a truly spectacular number of cultural shut-ins: generally speaking, Henry James, for theater people, is a man whose novel turned into *The Heiress,* T. S. Eliot is the author of *The Cocktail Party,* Edmund Wilson of *The Little Blue Light* and Gide the translator of *Hamlet.*

No doubt in one sense all this is obvious and even logical enough, for were there less ignorance, there couldn't be so many experts. And the essence of the expert is that his field shall be very special and narrow: one of the ways in which he inspires confidence is to rigidly limit himself to the little toe; he would scarcely venture an off-the-record opinion on an infected little finger. Such cautious specializing inspires confidence but rather makes for difficulties: the seeker after broad culture or an "integrated" point of view is very long in getting it; he is like someone who must stop every half hour at a new frontier and go through the customs, or like a blind man who every little while must ask help in crossing a new street, with the total experience being much that of the blind men and the elephant.

Recently I went to a conference called by a society of historians with a view to publishing a magazine that should deal with history. Various social scientists who were present — men in such fields as psychology, anthropology, sociology, government—offered their views. Though the reason for the get-together was a magazine that should make history interesting to large numbers of people, not a single social scientist who spoke saw history as a broad parent source, let alone a great cultural stream. Each one saw it merely in relation—when it was not in downright opposition—to his own subject. Each saw it, moreover, entirely in terms of education, knowledge, "skills." The psychologist confessed that in the past psychology had at times been forced, from desperation, to fall back on history, but he added, far more brightly, that its usefulness was now quite trifling and that very soon psychology would be able to disregard history altogether. Such attitudes—expressed, as it were, in the bosom of the family—were perhaps understandable enough. But considering the reason for the conference, it is hard to say which seemed more extraordinary—the almost complete neglect of the problem of a history magazine, or the uniform attitude toward history itself, as at best the merest flunky of one ology or another and a flunky that soon could be given the sack. But what was perhaps most interesting of all, not a single speaker offered one graphic or picturesque example, indulged once in a vivid or pungent figure of speech. All was data, agenda, curricula, phenomena, such phrases as "interdisciplinary approach," "material context," "historical continuum"— pure cultural Choctaw in a field that produced Thucydides and Tacitus, Gibbon and Parkman.* Each speaker had the whole conference's eggs in his own little basket; each basket was

* This applies only to the Social Science session; at a later one that I couldn't get to, I gather that the Humanities got in their licks at the expense of the Social Sciences.

plainly labeled either "Education" or "Knowledge" (though it is obvious that the finest possible "education" must be out of date within twenty years); while in culture there was not the faintest sign of interest.

The tragedy is that instead of valuably supplementing the general practitioner in all kinds of fields, the specialist has everywhere begun to drive him out. There are, of course, indispensable kinds of specialists—men whose methods of approach are scrupulously scientific, whose fields of operation are carefully defined, whose weapon is the fullest firsthand knowledge and who make of it the most soberly perceptive use. Such a man, let us say, is a cancer specialist.

Of course the scientific method need not be restricted to the sciences; it can be equally applied to problems involving factual knowledge in the field of the arts. A manuscript can be as rewardingly investigated as a malady; an old book can be X-rayed for symptoms just as the human body is. Corresponding here to our cancer specialist, with a subject hardly less stealthy or conjectural, is, say, an Alexander Pope specialist.

Already, however, there is an obvious difference. I don't mean one of relative usefulness—that cancer is a matter of life and death to the entire human race, and Pope a personal enthusiasm for a few dozen people. I mean that the cancer specialist, even where he may widen his field to venture opinions on climate or diet, on costume or exercise, remains concerned with the central problem, with the cause or prevention or cure of cancer. If he suggests that overeating or sexual indulgence tends to cause cancer, his is strictly a medical and in no way a moral judgment. But he is a rare Pope specialist who will confine himself— or for that matter be allowed to confine himself—to the facts, and the inferences to be drawn from them, about Pope. As a Pope scholar he is inevitably involved in much more than Pope scholarship. He is involved with not only how good or bad a penman but with how good or bad a writer Pope was; with not just the mere sense of any passage in his work, but with also its sensibility; not just with why something must be the wrong word as printed, but with why something else is the right word as thought up. Being an expert on Pope, he is soon called on to deal with Pope criticism and very likely to write some of his own. He may, to be sure, be a sound and even distinguished critic, though he equally may not. But whether distinguished or commonplace, he will understandably grow proprietary about Pope and will exert a prestige he has earned in one field in another field where he has earned none at all. In other words, though the cancer specialist may be full of theories, some of them quite erratic, and may reach conclusions that are often quite unsound, they will in some sense proceed out of his facts and can always be checked against them. But the Pope specialist can hardly not pass from providing statements about Pope to offering judgments about poetry, can hardly not stray from the field of scholarship to the field of art.

The distinction between something like cancer and something like Pope is fairly obvious. A much greater area of difficulty is that of the social sciences, where facts are less decisive than with pure science; where theories abound and quickly replace and supersede one another; and where there is often just human element enough, just sense enough of the human enigma, to cry out for humanistic judgments. But the reign of Data, the whole religion of Ph.Deism, seems far from ending: at the moment there is certainly no sign of a palace revolution or of any rough handling from the mob. Nominally a great age of scientific inquiry, ours has actually become an age of superstition about the infallibility of science; of almost mystical faith in its nonmystical methods; above all—which perhaps most explains the expert's sovereignty—of external verities; of traffic-cop morality and rabbit-test truth. The enormous value and validity of psychoanalysis doesn't demolish the fact that many astute men lived before Sigmund Freud. Indeed, the many things that sociology or anthropology or psychiatry *can* do go far toward making us feel that they can actually do anything. To know that in a crisis we can rely, that we indeed *must* rely, on the specialist is quite different from abject dependence on him in all winds and weathers; and more even than that he assumes something of the old God or Father image, he reflects our whole God-and-Mammon point of view. The expert is our most fashionably scientific figure, as up-to-the-minute as our plumbing, and he uses a set of tools—whether verbal, technical or therapeutic—that reflect American inventiveness generally. And he ministers to the mystery of things not in straightforwardly unintelligible Latin, but in new-fangled, semimeaningful, semi-intelligible jargon. Most of all—and perhaps most significantly of all—the expert himself constitutes that very symbol of success that others go to him to find the key for. His ability to salvage or refashion or reorient lives is neatly correlated, very often, with his ability to make money. The enormousness of his fees somehow bears witness to the enormousness of his learning. And his ministrations are calculated either to straighten you out so that you too can mount the golden ladder, or to persuade you that without keeping your hand in his you will totter and at length collapse.* He is, finally, the perfect answer for an age that can live by neither faith nor reason alone, that must put a kind of unquestioning faith in the omnipotence of reason.

The specialist represents the final stage of our *ad hominem* argument for education. There is also the comforting feeling that with the expert nigh we not only needn't unravel our difficulties but can actually tangle them further: the lawyer will think up a dodge, the doctor will know a drug, the tax man find a loophole, the journalist coin a phrase, the public-relations counsel devise an "out." All this represents a certain real gain. There are fewer outright quacks, though probably more borderline phonies, than there once were; the old primordial ignorance is gone. And the fact that scientific discoveries are so frequent, that scientific cures come so fast, necessarily imposes a vaguely scientific attitude on our everyday life. No single god or idol can be wholly venerated, for many a pill is no longer usable after three months—not only have its properties lost their force, but the prescription itself has lost its soundness. All the same, one must deplore the sorry new twist given the old idea that knowledge is power; the dehumanizing effects, the arid results of data worship, that

---

* I don't mean that this is a deliberate, or even unconscious, tactic on the part of the expert himself; it is, much of it, part of the *Zeitgeist*, much of it often part of the neurosis of the people who seek him out; and he would be indeed godlike if the worshipful attitude displayed toward him didn't subtly affect his feeling about his role.

can let history be carved up like some vanquished state at a peace conference—this strip ceded to anthropology and that to political science. At worst this absorption in what makes the clock tick creates an alarming lack of interest in how well it keeps time. There is so much greater a passion to explain things than to express them, and a curious belief that to call water H_2O constitutes an explanation. What word is oftener on our lips than *specialist* or *expert;* what would come more oddly than *connoisseur?* There is not only the strictly utilitarian—not to say purely self-seeking—interest in education, there is the crusade for a kind of living based on common-denominator uniformity and test-tube wisdom. Whatever may be the relative virtue of the tigers of wrath compared with the horses of instruction, the tigers today haven't even the status of contenders. There is no margin left for realizing that some things should be formal, as others are functional; that some things must be felt, as others should be analyzed; that some things are never out of date because they have never been in style. What kind of culture have we when we can be as sure where half our bright boys got their literary opinions as one clotheshorse can be sure where another got her hat? What kind of culture have we when we can be as certain, on entering a room, that the owners have used an interior decorator as a Latin teacher can be that a student is using a trot?

However huge the gain in education, culture plays no part—often indeed is allowed no place—in it. I use the two words as more antithetical than there is perhaps historical warrant for; but the words, except as counters, are unimportant; it is two attitudes, two aspirations, two ends to living that signify: it is that the thing I call education has been perverted from a means into an end, and the thing I call culture, which is the right true end, has been quite lost sight of. In any case, intelligence has been set apart from sensibility, almost in fact set at odds with it; and the vital need to stamp out anti-intellectualism in scientific and philosophic fields has bred the vicious corollary of overvaluing the intellect in artistic and aesthetic ones. This being an age of education, it is indeed one of light—glare and all; the shaded bulb, the mellow glow, of culture goes unesteemed. Educated people do quite literally speak the same language, but cultivated people often don't need to speak at all. All this is, of course, to simplify and even misstate; yet the fact remains that the whole trend toward the specialist, the whole march toward maximum efficiency, the whole theme of progress and "a better life for our children"— that all such aspects of contemporary American life, some of them self-seeking and others humanitarian, some demanding ruthlessness and others imposing decency, are too vigorously programmatic; they turn education into insurance policies or investment plans for the well-fed soul in the well-fed body, or, worse yet, for first gaining the world and then saving one's soul.

That the use of the mind, the reward of the senses, the experience and enjoyment of the arts, the urbanities of social intercourse—that all the best elements of civilized living should, in actual practice, no longer be much inculcated is scarcely deniable. Ours must be the first age whose great goal, on a nonmaterial plane, is no fufillment but adjustment; and perhaps just such a goal has served as maladjustment's weapon. One sometimes wonders whether educational methods haven't been turned around: whether there mightn't be more emphasis on discipline, and less on self-expression, in the early school years, and less on discipline and more on self-expression in the colleges and graduate schools. What good is there in abolishing grades on report cards if, a dozen years later, there is a frantic and agonized scramble for that cultural rubber stamp, a B.A.? And, the B.A. attained, there is the grim and fearsome struggle for higher degrees, culminating in the torture chamber of the Ph.D. "oral." Why frown on having youngsters write *"puella, puellae"* fifty times on the blackboard when ten years later their theses will probably be assessed on a basis of how many quotations from other writers they contain or how many footnotes they boast? And as things are now, isn't receiving a Ph.D. frequently as fatal, as sure sentence of death as being denied one?

The graduate school is of immense value; but as it currently operates, it seems at times a forcing house to fatten up mediocrity, and the mediocrity would by no means seem confined to the students. Professors of a wonderful self-importance would seem essential to the plan—professors who compel upon gifted candidates the most fiendishly dull or magnificently ill-suited of projects. We may also, I think, be permitted to ask what a Ph.D. should certify. It would seem oftenest useful to me as a sort of wicket gate, or toll bridge, to a life of scholarship: I quite honestly cannot conceive what bearing it has on an active career of teaching. In its very concentratedness it requires a man to give up years to study in a single, usually very narrow field—where, as a teacher, or writer, or critic, or student of literature he could spend the time far more profitably ranging much greater territory, and pastured in much richer grass. But doubtless, were the higher-degree system abolished, some even higher degree of methodology would replace it; and what seems most deplorable of all to me is the attitude of some of the men who preside over seminars and at length congregate for orals. I remember the sort of professor I deplore once asking a distinguished and quite unacademic colleague his opinion of a certain Ph.D. thesis. "I thought," said the colleague, "it was very good indeed; didn't you?" "Oh," said the first man, "I thought it very good for an M.A.—but for a Ph.D.!"

Happily there are modern and enlightened colleges, and there are getting to be more of them; but they are still too few. And doubtless, professors are discouraged from relaxing the prescribed graduate-school methods; have come to take a pretty grim view of the average graduate student; see him as a symbol of *All hope abandon,* a specimen of *All passion spent.* So very many people must come to teaching, and with no real talent for it, for the sad reason that by the time they come to it they suspect that they have no great talent for anything else. So many, again, must find in the very drudgery of their research, in the very pedantry of their judgments, in the very pointlessness of their projects, a blessing in disguise: that which to the lively, fertile mind would seem a ghastly cul-de-sac must strike the grubbing plodder as the one avenue of his difficulties. To know all that *can* be known of Castiglione's influence on English courtesy books, or of Beaumont's collaborative habits with Fletcher (and far more restricted

subjects have been pitched upon), must give these grub-
bers a great sense of security in their findings and of
primacy in their field. And the work they do has its very
real uses, which one would genuinely thank them for
were it not that their rather specialized knowledge, and
the Ph.D. it has brought them, makes them into full professors and even heads of departments; lets them, like as
not, mishandle, misrepresent, dehydrate the masters af
literature they lecture on, and bore, bewilder, under-
nourish the students who sit listening.

But the tide is slowly beginning to turn. When, a year
or so ago, writing of how great a teacher "Copey" had
been at Harvard, but of how for lack of higher degrees he
had failed of formal advancement, Lewis Gannett depre-
cated, much as I do, the need of such degrees, he got
considerable enlightening mail. He was informed of how
many men without academic decorations, and often without college degrees, now teach or lecture in various colleges and universities. More and more, whether at the
great established colleges like Harvard and Princeton or
at such smaller and younger ones as Bennington, Brandeis,
Sarah Lawrence, the desire (often amounting to a policy)
is for people who not only know their subject but know
something beyond it, know something of general culture
and of human beings. And perhaps I should say what
one might suppose needed no saying: that there is a very
large number of excellent teachers, and even of people who
were clearly born to teach.

But all too often the opposite still holds true; and the
ends of a liberal, which is to say a liberating, culture are
being thwarted. The academic note, so far from being
confined to classroom and campus, is spreading outward,
is infecting policies and methods, is eating into criticism,
is indeed preying upon art. Great writers are being put
under the microscope as though they were interesting
diseases.* Yet, sadder even than that such tight-lipped
pleasure-shunning, punditlike methods exist is the fact
that, in view of something worse, they must almost at times

---

* Which, no doubt, they often are; but this aspect of them might better be
treated in courses in pathology, or at least be no more than indicated in courses
in literature. Nor is this because I wish to take a cheery view of life; it is only
because I—on a purely selfish basis—refuse to take a medical view of art.

be defended. For far worse, I think, than treating history and literature as forms of biochemistry is treating them as a form of intellectual bingo. Where the academic method dehydrates and medicates culture, a widespread journalistic approach forever spikes or sweetens it: instead of the laboratory and the reform school, we get the cocktail lounge and the vaudeville show. To reach the book counter in one or two literary journals, one must push one's way through the toy department, the radio and TV department, the quiz show conducted in the ladies' millinery, the jam session featured in the men's furnishings, the line of people cashing in their box tops to acquire the latest kitchen gadget. Nor, when one finally reaches the book counter, is there a very rewarding display.

We thus have two fights on our hands. It is plain that one must never abuse the academics as a way of giving aid to the philistines and the playboys, but it is just as plain that one cannot spare them, either. For one thing, they are frequently as hostile to art, to the broad free spirit of culture, as are the philistines themselves. At best, they have carried into art some of the more understandable attitudes of education—such as a special fondness for the problem child; such as an urge to *make* a problem child of the reasonably normal or pleasantly talented one. It is bad enough to break a butterfly on a wheel, but with these people we have often the spectacle of laboriously setting up the wheel without ever breaking the butterfly. One wonders just how good they can be at artistic solid geometry after giving them an easy sum—like Scott Fitzgerald—to do and seeing them arrive at so wrong an answer. Our pundits suggest, to me, those doctors who are too anxious to operate: many of their patients don't need surgery, while others can get no help from it. Worst of all, this constant recourse to the X ray and the operating table is no offset to the jaunty bedside manner and sugar-water prescriptions of the intellectual-bingo school. We are left helpless between one group that makes a serious problem of everything and another that provides a comforting answer, between those who insist that every nursery rhyme is profound symbolism and those who assure you that James Joyce is mere nonsense.

Accordingly, in an America that either imbibes art frivolously through a straw or is fed it, while gasping for breath, through a tube, the old humanistic traditions, the classic aesthetic values, have gone tragically out of fashion and to a great extent out of use. The Muses have vanished, giving way to the mineralogists and the medical corps, while the New Criticism, despite its self dedication to masterpieces, is no real counterweight to the ism-haunted and ology-infested scene; for though the New Critics refuse to excavate, they themselves, at times, seem to live underground or, more accurately, inside diving bells. The imagination itself has been so persistently intellectualized that our age has developed a brand-new instinct—a determined instinct to resist instinct, to denounce, discredit, expel it. At the higher levels of much of our criticism mere responsiveness is judged of no account, while such other arts as painting and music, with their valuable corroborative responses, their testimony about form, their own innate qualities of verve, vitality, style, possess no standing as witnesses, are seldom, indeed, called into the witness box.

It has always been this interpenetration of the arts—in contrast with *our* new entanglement with the sciences— that has given to European culture its richness and breadth and that has made its representative critics into, as it were, cultural men-about-town, men equally at home in the library, the concert hall, the opera house, the art gallery, the salon—and the night club and sidewalk café. It was for this air of Continental culture that a generation of Americans, from Huneker to Carl Van Vechten and Stark Young, possessed a special value. They were ciceroni, they helped liberate many Americans from provincial ignorance or national prejudice, they stimulated many Americans to go farther or dig deeper; they performed the role, among various arts, that Edmund Wilson was to perform more decisively among various literatures. As a result, those of us who were young in the 20s, however cocky or frivolous we might be, were not—like the young of today—in bondage to the pundits; we were rather in contemptuous and militant revolt against them. It has taken some thirty years for the heroes of every clever undergraduate of the '20s to become the sacred cows and petted lap dogs of present-day academics. I remember, around 1923, writing a piece for an English course on *Women in Love* and being told I had far better have chosen Galsworthy; while the head of the English department used to refer to "that man Menn-kin." To such men all our gods—Joyce, Proust, Lawrence, the Eliot of *The Waste Land*—were either anathema or highly suspect; Flaubert, for them, was farthest north on the map, we had to discover Stendhal for ourselves. Professors, I would think, are better today—or at any rate extol finer writers—but young people, whom they have in bondage, are worse. I am old-fashioned enough to think that the young should break ground, heave rocks, smash idols, even create a perceptible amount of damage. The young are immemorially intolerant and intransigent, and they are quite entitled to be—so long as they explore and experiment for themselves. But today's pursed-lipped snobs and name-droppers, too much at the feet and too little at the throats of their elders, seem to me depressingly unadventurous; if, often, they don't revolt in the name of sense, they ought to in the name of style.

"Close thy Byron: open thy Goethe"— the reverse injunction almost seems called for at the moment. Shut thy textbooks, fling the nineteenth critical volume on Herman Melville out the window and put a Rossini overture on the gramophone, go hear *Carmen,* look at Daumier. Put first things first: know what verve, and freshness, and energy are, and how enchanting they can be. Sample mere genius for a change. Never fear: Art always knows its real friends from its fair-weather ones; it knows who sticks by Heine or Hardy, Molière or Cervantes, Landor or Turgenev in their adversity, while all the world has gone to call on Kafka or Kierkegaard; it knows who sits at Wordsworth's or Tennyson's bedside when they are given up for dead. Art even knows those who, for all their obsequious fuss, aren't even its fair-weather friends, aren't friends of any kind. Prig and philistine, Ph.D. and C.P.A., despot of English 218c and big shot of the Kiwanis Club—how much, at bottom, they hate Art, and how hard it is to know which of them hates it the more.

TWO

1. The Decline of Sensibility

THERE has been a certain improvement during the last hundred years in the way people conduct themselves toward such other people as they need not be polite to. To decide whether Americans have as good manners today as they did in the past would involve the whole question of what good manners are and of whether what once seemed *de rigueur* isn't now just stuffy or elaborate. Manners today are permissibly so much freer, small punctilios are so generally unobserved, that it is often hard to distinguish between the rude and the sloppy, the deliberate slur and the thoughtless slight. About all we still can say is that certain people have breeding and others don't; and we would surely agree that a highbred tradition, far from being well maintained, is seldom even much desired; that whatever it may constitute for the common man, ours is clearly the century of the common manner.

But all that is part of *autres temps, autres moeurs* and has little to do with the run of human relationships, with how much ease, civility and friendly give-and-take now obtains in American life. In ease, civility and friendly give-and-take there has been, I think, a decided gain. Even those who scarcely pay lip service to democracy must, in most relationships, adjure haughtiness and putting on airs. For they are aware that if they don't, they may be more than just frowned on; they may be laughed at. Indeed, most relationships in America, whether between families and servants, or bosses and employees, or housewives and shopkeepers, show little calculated rudeness or outright condescension. Position in America rests on acquired forms of power far more than on ingrained forms of privilege, for it is power, not privilege, that we respect. Boorishness that shows strength and character can impress us, where upper-class haughtiness makes us snicker. Even what seems to me our most obnoxious American type—which is not the parvenu but the smug upper-middle-class city dweller who has been heaped with advantages but not even tinctured with *noblesse oblige*—even these people, who sail into shops, can't be kept waiting, expect special attention, want a three-dollar book delivered by special messenger to the *Queen Mary,* even such as these have learned just how far they can go. For "unreasonable" people have been fingerprinted; the boss himself in such cases is on the side of the salesgirl. There is no longer in America (if there ever was) a special way of being rude to one's inferiors.

In fact, it is almost the other way round: it is a proof—or at any rate a pretense—of American equality that you lose your temper as freely with your office boy as with your partner; it is a testimonial of how man-to-man we are that we call a truck driver a son of a bitch instead of coldly glaring at him; or forget, rather than remember, to bid an assistant good morning. The decline, if not indeed the collapse, of punctilios has, I feel sure, prevented far more pain than it has caused. Formerly, if a man forgot to perform some established bit of office ritual, or did something one Christmas and not the next, he could disconcert and upset a great many people, make them feel they had been deliberately snubbed, even make them uneasy about their jobs. Today there is much less ritual and much less concern over it. And though there is a good deal of upstartism and big-shotism and rank-pulling in American life, insolence is exceedingly rare. It is largely Anglophiles who cultivate it: it is no more a part of our tradition than it is in our blood. The boss's son is made to start, almost ostentatiously, at the bottom and is taught above everything else—since it serves Mammon and Demos equally well—to mingle. Even our worst roughnecks in power, our recentest beggars on horseback, learn fast that though they can fairly safely brag, they can seldom safely bully.

However sloppy manners are today, there is less high-handedness, less calculated cruelty, than there once was; and what little there is seems based less on social snobbery than on personal or institutional self-importance; on being so deep in thought in the elevator, so involved with problems in the corridor, so harried by decisions in the men's washroom as to have no more than a nod for whomever one meets. What the institutional big shot exudes is no simple odor of caste, but a portentous air of destiny.

Actually, what is now corrupting human relations at the more professional and intellectual levels of American life is not aloofness, condescension or snobbery, but a tremendous increase in familiarity. It is not the so-called leveling process itself (with its mixture of good and bad) that calls for study here but the *exploitation* of this leveling process. Against the gain in surface democracy and friendliness must be noted a sharp decline in sensibility. Against the old, all-but-vanished exploitation of one's own status must be set the new, ever-increasing exploitation of the other guy's good nature. If formerly one gave too little among one's associates and acquaintances, today one asks too much. If formerly the person of lesser "rank" was the victim of exclusion, he is today the victim of invasion. I am thinking only of those social areas where sensibility can be supposed to exist, where delicacy of approach might be thought traditional. This is not to proclaim where, or where not, such sensibility is actually found. Many dowagers —as we all know—conspicuously lack it, many dishwashers plainly possess it: my point here is that there are milieus where sensibility is assumed to be the guiding thread—in contrast to the established etiquettes that govern more standardized living. Thus sensibility, since it rests on imagination and understanding, is properly looked for in the "artist." Sensibility must be as carefully distinguished from goodheartedness on the one hand as from good form on the other: goodhearted people often quite lack delicacy, as exemplars of good form quite lack feeling. Hence most writers, even those without much talent, have possessed a good deal of sensibility. They may be banal or inelegant or even crude as writers, but they are not often philistines. They may lack *savoir-faire,* they may be sullen or boorish or gauche, but they are not gross or coarse-grained. And something of this sensibility has always existed among people who, whether they were creative or artistic, were exposed to a truly humanistic—as opposed to a merely genteel—culture.

The decline in such finer feeling is today very marked. A very great number of people still, of course, display it, but for a variety of reasons there are much fewer such people than there might be. To begin with, there has been a general sloughing off of what are classically known as the amenities. Again, there is the coarsening effect of contemporary life, with its brutal and jostling competitiveness, its *sauve-qui-peut*-ism. There is finally the emergence of a whole new, powerful, ubiquitous class who have gone far beyond "commercializing" art forms, who quite simply regard them as out-and-out merchandise, a class whose identification might seem to be with professional ethics and artistic interests but is actually with business and business methods.

This last phenomenon is very important. The huge growth and spread of radio, television, advertising, publicity, movies, photography, scenic design, interior decoration and all the applied and industrial arts have made words, sounds, colors, designs as much of an industry and as vast a one as railroads or machine parts. Great numbers of people make their livings through a creative knack, through cleverness, talent, skill—word juggling, tune-making, storytelling—and at the same time function completely as businessmen.* Nor is this, as it is often made out to be, simply a matter of circumstances. It is equally one of inner desire: most such people aren't even split personalities or "frustrated" artists. It was not very long

* The businessman attitude remains a matter of inner psychology and ultimate aims, not just of habits or working methods or the natural desire for material success. Trollope worked like a unionized skilled laborer and wrote no doubt for a definite market; but he was only a curiously businesslike writer, not a literary businessman.

ago that every seedy, drunken newspaperman gabbled of the novel he was writing or meant to write; that bright youngsters out of college took jobs because they had to, but dreamed of Paris and Picasso, or Bloomsbury, or the Village. Back in the '20s an unknown writer who couldn't afford the luxury of a purely "creative" career was even hard put to it to find a halfway-right job: he could teach, or land one of a very limited number of jobs on magazines or in publishing houses, or perhaps work in a bookstore, or do book reviewing or research. It was scarcely easier to succeed as a hack than as an artist. Today one increasingly meets young people who aren't resigned to making good at their jobs but are resolved upon it. They virtually decided to commercialize their talents before they were out of college. Where my generation was writing poetry or critical essays, these youngsters are studying radio scripts or casing TV shows: the sedulous ape is now someone who enters his name in the rat race. And even at the outset, these people seem to see no difference, seem to make no choice between a distinguished career and a successful one. They don't compromise, as so many people must, or capitulate, as so many finally do, or become obvious victims of economic pressure. They don't sell out; they are exultant volunteers. They are a new species, a new race, for whom all the counters of art are the mere tools of industry.

They happen, a great many of them, to be young people with neither cultural nor social backgrounds. But the effect of this is almost the reverse of what it used to be. Formerly the bright, "sensitive" kids who came from modest or struggling households—the children of Jewish, Irish, Italian immigrants, the factory workers who went to night school, the scholarship kids at college — formerly these, all the more for what was lacking at home, had a fierce love of learning for its own sake, of poetry or painting or music for what they brought to life. One need not sentimentalize them; all too many had only the thinnest talent, all too many had been warped as human beings. But they were not hard and assured and cocky; and however boisterously intolerant or self-righteously proletarian, they were almost to a man antiphilistine. They were among the most sensitive people one met.

The new species is among the most insensitive. It cynically confesses all (and thereafter protests nothing) by dubbing its struggle a rat race. It has no sense of having ever been coarsened or corrupted; it is prevulgarized, as materials are said to be preshrunk. These people, as a class, display much more than mere intelligence or talent; they display a good deal of "right thinking"; they aren't necessarily illiberal; and where such things as living, housing, education, racial discrimination are concerned, they are altogether enlightened. Nor are they overtly hard-boiled. Rather, they have a briskly informal relationship toward others, which exhibits a strong touch of the good fellow and a complete absence of the stuffed shirt. The whole atmosphere they live in, the whole atmosphere they create, is one that encourages the taking of small liberties, the sloughing off of niceties and scruples. When they are asking a favor, when they are seeking information they have no right to, or when, again, they are refusing *you* a favor or treating you a little treacherously, they drape the moment in humor or blandly confess their crime. In a sense, all this is of a piece with sport shirts, no bathing-suit tops, single-unit livingroom-diningroom-kitchens and all the other things that have destroyed formality and false shame.

But one of the misfortunes of our time is that in getting rid of false shame we have killed off so much real shame as well. Even so, the middle class, formerly knee-deep in the proprieties, formerly enslaved by Mrs. Grundy, may have gained far more than it lost—but not those for whom informality is one thing and intrusiveness another, false refinement one thing and right feeling another. With this emerging new race it is almost axiomatic to have no genteel shibboleths, to subscribe to no useless repressive forms. But, in destroying barriers, they have lost all sense of boundaries; they don't seem to know—though I suspect they know only too well—the difference between not standing on ceremony with people and taking advantage of them. Let me give a fairly mild example. A few years ago a writer whom I never knew well and hadn't seen or heard from for years wrote to me that by the same mail he was sending me a ms. which he would like me to read. "I'm not first asking your permission," he went on to say, "because I know that if I did, you might damn well not give it." This is the frank, informal tone to use, the humorously outrageous technique.

And all the more outrageous, because it is so trifling, is the whole business of first names. To go at it a little obliquely, there is—for one thing—the recent but already ubiquitous custom, among this new race, of addressing perfect strangers as "Dear William Smith." Temperamentally, I happen to find the custom loathsome because it even *sounds* ugly and unnatural. As a special kind of salutation it has, to be sure, a considerable history. Henry James might write to a very much younger man (because he knew the man's family and because, one might add, he was Henry James) "Dear Mr. Arthur Benson," and then drop the "Mr." before dropping the "Benson"; and on occasion, from having friends in common or a sort of equal public standing, people might address other people they had not met as "Dear Harry Jones." But this was a way of saying "We aren't really strangers," where the usage today is a forcible way of confessing we are; for, at the first meeting or by the second letter, these people shift to the straight-out use of first names. Many of them are not yet twenty-five years old. I very much doubt that they mean to be presumptuous; I very much imagine that they wish to be correct. And as this is the common coin of their elders and superiors, it seems right out of Emily Post.

One of the melancholy effects of this decline of sensibility is that as a tasteless and perhaps not quite guileless informality increases, its victims develop a streak of the priggish and old-fashioned. I don't think it's from any silly notions of dignity or self-importance that many people resent, for example, this use of first names. In offices, in organizations, wherever people are habitually thrown together, the prompt use of first names is not only natural in itself but prevents difficulties and awkwardness later. But a man who has no conceivable right, who indeed has no conceivable reason, to call you by your first name must, in doing so, offend some sleeping sense of the stiff-necked in you. And for that matter, if a man can call you by your first name, he has you at an unfair advantage. In the eyes of the world, he has some small claim on you which you, at the cost of seeming ungracious or even treacherous, may be forced to deny. First-naming may be a mere phase, of a piece with women in Jane Austen's time addressing men by their last names, but the one strikes as false and familiar a note as the other.

I use first-naming as a symptom and a symbol, not because it matters much in itself. What I would stress is that it is only because sensibility operates as an inner check, only because taste is at the controls, that the professional or emancipated classes can dispense with conventions. But it is surely plain that unconventionality involves a finer tact than conventional good form does—just as two people who are living together must show more such tact than two who are married. But what, among the professional classes, one finds more and more common is a want of conventional good manners and of personal sensibility alike.

The two things, of course—sensibility and "good form" —tend to operate on almost opposite lines. So-called good society, since it is largely based on *ignoring* the source of most wealth, the blots on most scutcheons, the skeletons in most closets and the uglier and more unsavory facts of life, has long considered it bad form to talk openly about money, ailments, dubious antecedents or the realities of sex, and to avert one's eyes from all but the most respectable and universal of misfortunes. The professional and emancipated classes accept the uglier facts of life, the sordid origins of wealth, the black sheep and the bulbous noses; and though even they might shy away from the fact that a friend's father was lynched or his sister could regularly be seen accosting sailors after nightfall, they would certainly not display that tact (which is really gross tactlessness) of side-stepping what stared them in the face, of never mentioning a friend's brother who drank or father who failed in business, nor would the possessor of such kinsmen himself be stuffy or touchy about them. The professional classes, for the most part, feel no hesitation asking any sensible question for any sound reason—from the rent on summer cottages to the results obtained at sanatoriums for alcoholics or at schools for retarded children. Sensibility not only accepts the facts of life; it is all the more concerned with maintaining decency because the facts are so often ugly. But where sensibility fails to function, conventional good manners become the only way left to keep from having our egos assailed or our good nature imposed upon.

The previous generation—the age of jazz, of Prohibition, of Greenwich Village; of shrugging shoulders, crashing gates and smashing idols—introduced some very attractive forms of license. Hence the bored rich, far more eager to be amused than be exclusive, established Café Society. The new race that I have been speaking of—most of them new-rich or on the way to being—have, for their own use, appropriated many of Café Society's assumptions and habits. Some of them, in time, become part of that society, but even before that they have a frequent curbstone, or bar-rail, or sixth-row-center view of it; it is perhaps not entirely fantastic to suppose that this new race has picked up much of its etiquette on such highbred occasions as a fashionable opening night. They have perhaps seen, as I have, Miss Elsa Maxwell, on a raw snowy evening, just before curtaintime, hold court right in the bottleneck entrance of a theater, greeting and throwing her arms about her acquaintance, and keep others on the sidewalk in the snow. Or, thanks to Leonard Lyons, one may read of the guests at the publicist Mr. Benjamin Sonnenberg's dinner parties:

> Dorothy Stickney was one of the dinner guests last night at the home of the Ben Sonnenbergs. The host always briefs his guests about those who are to be their dinner partners. So that Miss Stickney would know about Alistair Cooke, who would be seated at her right, he sent the star a copy of Cooke's newest book, "One Man's America." He also sent Miss Stickney a $1 bill, money to typify the man who would be seated at her left, Winthrop Rockefeller.

It is perhaps sentimental in one, but there would seem to have been a kind of wholesome straightforward misbehavior about the days of one's youth. In those childish times people sitting next to you at dinner would pass right out in the midst of telling an anecdote; and very tactful it was of them, since with their drunken blather they were crashing bores. In those days people might have a sudden desire to strip: I remember one woman who undressed, during the fish course, to show everyone an exotic jewel she was wearing in her navel. Or they might make rather unseemly love in public. But they at least had the decency to make fools or boors or spectacles of *themselves,* and they took advantage of nothing worse than the other fellow's time or patience. Moreover, there was a kind of poetic justice about it all: their bad manners were directed toward ruining their careers, not furthering them; at worst, their misdeeds made nursemaids of their acquaintances, not steppingstones; and the philosophy they preached was that of the primrose path and not of the main chance. And though, after a fifth or sixth cocktail—the very recipes for which would induce queasiness today—one might Tell All about oneself, even then one didn't ask too much about other people. Next morning one perhaps called up the hostess to apologize for such inconvenience as one had caused her—the stained slip cover, the smashed plate, the guest one had poked in the eye; now one phones a stranger one met the night before to "confirm" that lunch date or remind him to send those letters of introduction. There was something nice to an age when people never grew up, compared with one in which they have no youth, in which, already in their early twenties, people are slick, calculating, career-minded. A sort of pristine pathos hovers about him who in time sells out: selling out argues a period of idealism or integrity, a moment, however botched, of moral crisis. But this new breed experiences no such crisis; there is no struggle; they don't sell out at 40, they sign up at 22. One can even at moments understand why there are now, along with so many shameless young careerists, so many tight-lipped young prigs: they are sitting full-time, in judgment on a society that cries out to be judged.

And the '20s—so far as the bright young men, the clever young talents, the enlightened professional classes were concerned—could boast, by comparison with today, more than a picturesque sloppiness. The bright and the clever may have set a bad example with their often splotchy bohemianism, their comic defiances, their phony cults, their alcoholic and vagabond irresponsibility. But they were lined up squarely on the side of art and not on the side of money. Even artiness, unbearable as it can be, is the homage that pretension renders to talent. And the '20s were pervasively "literary": the middle class had its *American Mercury* quite as much as the intellectuals their *Dial* and *transition*. In a society of drunks, certain niceties had by 10:00 P.M. necessarily disappeared; but if, in the '20s, more men stole one another's wives, fewer stole each other's jobs. It's not that in the moral sense the '20s didn't badly call for improvement. It's that things, in the moral sense, can hardly be thought to have improved.

2. A Note on Privacy

WE who are old enough to have seen the loss of privacy come about can truly deplore the lack of it. But how will future generations feel? Will they so much as be aware of what has vanished? There is perhaps a connection between the destruction of privacy and the breakdown, somewhat earlier, of genteel restraints. It stands to reason that in the days when certain things weren't openly talked about—whether in so-called good society, or between the sexes, or in the presence of the young—people enjoyed considerable privacy because their bad habits and misdeeds were so little discussed. Doubtless the very famous and the exceedingly high-placed have always lived in glass houses; and if, indeed, the King can do no wrong, what harm in mentioning his friendships with opera singers? Doubtless, too, there have always been whispering campaigns and scandal sheets; in an age, moveover, when love affairs were more clandestine, there was something more scandalous about their coming to light. And in an age of relatively few divorces, such ones as there were would cause more talk—and more whispers. But so long as the gamier facts of life were deemed unsuited to public knowledge, the gaudier private histories could be largely curtained off. In an age when the *jeune fille bien élevée* knew little of what went on after marriage, she naturally knew even less of what went on outside it. In an age when it was considered bad form to refer to people's respectable diseases, it must have been quite unthinkable to discuss their unseemly ones. No doubt tongues have always wagged, but that is by no means to specify what they wagged over. Where in one age it might be because a young girl carried her own latchkey, in another it might mean she carried one to a young man's flat. In earlier periods, at any rate, references were usually veiled and rumors indefinite.

But as people became more emancipated and thence more outspoken; as, shedding various fears and shames, they demanded less privacy for themselves, they became a little less punctilious about respecting the privacy of others. With a loss of mere gentility went the loss, too, of a certain delicacy. Referring, in a humorous way, now to themselves, now to other people, they came in time to throw off reserves along with repressions. In these matters, of course, even more decisive than the things one may tell are the things one may ask: it is perhaps on this, more than on any other single matter, that a really sensitive society depends. Doubtless a good general rule for close friendships, where confidences are freely exchanged, is that what one is not informed about one may not inquire about. But in an age of interviewers, of gossip columnists, of TV confessions and camera exposés, people have not only developed a quite new kind of curiosity about the private lives of strangers; by contamination with so much professional prying they have come to pry more and more among their own friends.

What is perhaps strangest today is the keen widespread interest displayed toward people who are, on the one hand, not real celebrities and, on the other, not personally known to one. Most gossip that doesn't concern one's friends and acquaintances has, classically, a certain snob appeal— has to do with people of great wealth or fame or beauty. But much that one reads today in the gossip columns has to do, it might almost be said, with people whose reputations are being made at the same time they're being unmade—people who only exist, as it were, in terms of the gossip. The who's-dating-whom, the rumors of divorce, the shifts of affection, the speculations as to marriage, the pregnancies and births are for the most part—in New York, at any rate—about people only marginally in the limelight and often actually on the side lines. That Sonny Tink, the underwear heir, is dating a starlet, or even a showgirl; that a TV scriptwriter is horning in on the happy home of a candy-bar maker; that it's a boy at the Gumbridges (his pajama company sponsors a minor radio program); that a dog-biscuit tycoon has taken to investing in Broadway shows—this is the run of such stuff; and in a city of 8,000,000 people—a city that teems with real celebrities—this would seem to me of a piece with the trailer items in an old-fashioned small-town society column. But it would seem to me to lack the society column's pertinence (in a small town one knows or cares more about the people), or the society column's provincial charm (how ripping that Mrs. Cogswell entertained with a bridge-tea to display her new living-room suite). It is one of the sublime provincialities of New York that its inhabitants lap up trivial gossip about essential nobodies they've never set eyes on, while continuing to boast that they could live somewhere for twenty years without so much as exchanging pleasantries with their neighbors across the hall.

An age of publicity cannot but make privacy first difficult and at length undesirable: eventually people, if they can feel sure that everyone will know their address, will cheerfully live in glass houses. People will even hanker after glass houses, will suffer from a glass-houses compulsion derived not from an innate exhibitionism but from an acquired competitiveness. Being gossiped about— of course not too calamitously or too drably—may be an extreme way, but is also an effective one, of becoming known to the nobbier maîtres d'hôtel or the snootier *couturiers,* or of being nodded to at first nights or deferred to at benefits or race tracks; and often getting one's picture in the news columns is the quickest way, or the only way, of getting it into the society columns. Privacy, today, is accounted even less of an asset than a virtue.

The moment would seem to me a truly critical one. The real unconcern for privacy that has already, with the present generation, come to seem normal will inside a dozen or fifteen years be taken so completely for granted as to pose no social problem or engender no personal qualms. However revolted most people of sensibility may still be by all this, they are no longer, certainly, much shocked; and what people begin to expect, and then come to accept, of others they must gradually begin to adopt for themselves. Evil communications corrupt good manners; but that's not the whole of it. What *were* good manners can come to seem priggish ones. Moreover, even people whose manners still *are* good, whose sensibilities still serve them as controls, lead—in a perfectly legitimate sense—far more public lives than they would once have done. The legislators, the clergymen, the professors, the editors, the writers —all the policy makers of our life, as it were—are constantly heard on the radio and seen on TV, are recurrently interviewed and round-tabled and forumized and questionnaired. The sixteen-year-olds in their children's schools summon them to the high-school auditorium to ask them questions that once upon a time they would not only have never dared ask their own parents but that would never have entered their minds. Our public figures are already at ease in a world their fathers could not have visualized; and the more public their lives are made, the more confused must they be as to what constitutes privacy.

As for radio and TV, half their "social-thinking" and "public-welfare" programs seem to center in people— usually quite ordinary people—with pasts, or with plights, or with problems. Where once people wrote anonymously to Beatrice Fairfax, they now appear on *Guess My Secret* or *What's My Vice?* persuaded that, however bacchic or narcotic, or larcenous or libertine or steeped-in-blood their lives may be, the willingness to Tell All is as exculpatory as it will be curative. And if so many different people, for so many different reasons, are willing to tell all, the fact must, first, encourage others to do likewise; and then a bit later make them feel that it is rather shameful *not* to do likewise; and ultimately embolden them not only to tell all themselves but to ask all of others. Quite soberly I would suggest that the gradual breakdown of the old ordinary resistances, the rendering it "normal" to tell more and more private facts in more and more public circumstances, is something that must render counterarguments futile. In the run of superior people the desire for publicity created by the ego is offset by a dislike of it—in its cruder forms, at any rate—fostered by their taste. Such people, first by instinct, later on principle, will hold out against being vulgarized all they can. But once a questionable procedure comes to be not just accepted practice but—after a while—completely normal and "right," the superior person must not only, in following his own canons of taste, become something of a martyr; by other people's standards he must seem something of a prig. Indeed, a sort of countermorality begins to obtain. Thus, Mr. and Mrs. Danny Kaye carefully issue a statement to the press concerning their "trial" separation; to avoid trying to explain such a move would presumably seem illiberal; to be reserved in such a matter would smack of being reactionary. In a world of moral nudism, wearing clothes doesn't just mean that you're prudish; it suggests that you may have something to hide.

Here join hands, I think, the two key figures of the age—the press agent and the psychoanalyst. Here the careerist need for publicity is given aid and comfort through the human need for confession. Talking about oneself, talking oneself up, Telling All are not just egocentric but therapeutic. However ignorant or misinformed the man in the street may be about psychiatry, he is fully aware that repressions can be dangerous. Hence such things as "reserve" and "privacy" are less to be cherished than feared; while, career- or reputation-wise once it becomes known that you go to an analyst, how can why you go matter? Indeed, you almost have to tell why you go in self-defense, lest it be thought—and then whispered, and then known for a fact—that you go for something very dark and dreadful. Willingly or not, the analyst himself is by now a leading figure in the gossip columns; no sooner is the public informed in whose bed So-and-So reclines than it is told on whose couch. What with the gossip item so spotlighted on the one hand and the case history on the other—what with opening one's house to the photographers, one's past to the syndicates, one's plight to the microphones, one's domestic life to the divorce courts, and on those terms becoming a newpaper headliner and a national heroine—any surviving desire for privacy will not only drive one to the poorhouse; it may well expose one to the lunacy commission, or even to the law.

3. The New New-Rich

ONE very real social phenomenon of our time is that "creative" people constitute America's newest *nouveaux riches*. There are astonishingly many book and magazine writers, playwrights, librettists, writers for the movies, for radio, for TV, actors and directors, lecturers and columnists, song writers and musical-comedy composers, public-relations men, commercial artists, designers, editors, consultants and the like who earn more—usually a great deal more—than say, $75,000 a year. To be sure, most of them are people with big earning capacities rather than established incomes or solid fortunes. Numerically, all the same, they are an imposing group; personally, they are so well known as to be a particularly spotlighted one; and since the bulk of them are associated with either New York or Hollywood, they play a tremendous role in the social life of those communities.

So far as I know, there has never been anything exactly comparable to this. Even allowing for the actors, singers and virtuosos who earned large fortunes in the past, for the few great writers—Scott, Dickens, Mark Twain and the many more popular ones who managed to live *en prince,* never were there enough such people at any one time to be regarded as a class; nor were they ever compact and "established" enough to constitute a society. The best of them might be sought out, lionized, courted, petted, spoiled —a Pope in one age, a Sir Joshua or a Sir Walter in another. But ten such men were definitely patronized for every one who actually hobnobbed with his patrons; and though the fortunate among them might climb or marry into the upper classes, they never constituted a reigning social class themselves.*

The first such special society to emerge was, of course, Hollywood. But the great Hollywood incomes were a race apart: such people constituted a "society" by virtue of constituting an industry and by virtue, again, of being the only local society that existed. Hollywood, after all, was—on however grand a scale—a company town. Hollywood's was also a society altogether without roots, traditions or standards, and without connections anywhere else: it was a boom town that just happened to gush treacle rather than oil. It soon acquired the stigmata of a true caste system, based completely on one's particular title and wage. It equally became the most flagrant caricature of a society: its crudities and enormities of living and entertaining, of dress and decoration and architecture, became national jokes; its Goldwynisms became the hallmark of its culture; its great men—the heads of its great studios—cast a kind of *slur* on greatness.

All the same, Hollywood was the first huge and yet centralized industry that had a basic need of every variety of creative talent. It was the first occasion for thousands of writers, actors, directors, designers, costumers and technicians to operate exactly as might an equal number of skilled workers in cloth or soap. It was the first time that entertainment was created on an international mass-market scale, and that a man's ability to gauge the sales returns of a cops-and-robbers plot paid off much as another man's to gauge the sales returns of a particular kind of car carburetor or brassiere. Most significantly for the future, however, it was the first time that great numbers of "creative" people worked more or less regularly in a single community for extremely high pay. The people of talent who went to Hollywood just before and during the '20s were the pioneers of a new plutocracy. Earlier, no doubt, there had been some dozens of writers scattered through the country who, by their plays or novels or magazine writings or syndicated copy, had large incomes, but by comparison

---

* There have always, of course, been artists who were born to wealth or position, but they oftener rebelled or drifted away from the great world than remained part of it; and in no case did they constitute a *group* of creative rich people.

they were scanty in number and widely scattered about. (On the *creative* side, Broadway never had a large number of big money-makers at any one time.)

A true plutocracy of talent, unknown and quite unfore-seeable in 1900, had established itself—but in Hollywood alone—by 1925. But before 1950 a comparable society was flourishing in New York on far less primitive lines. Well-to-do talent had indeed reached the second stage of prosperity and a new style of living: rather than buying places in Bucks County or Westport, they were more and more disposing of them to middle-class liberals; they had made Beekman Place and the lower East Sixties not only their own, but often more expensive than Fifth or Park Avenue. They had made the fortune of "21," of John-Frederics, of Valentina; they had become the headlines half of Café Society, supplying the brains and talent where more established (though not necessarily very distin-guished) names supplied the blood. But where money was concerned, honors in Café Society were easy. Café Society contributed, indeed, an interesting new wrinkle: the rich who formerly offered the talented a glimpse of high life on condition that they sing for their suppers, now induced them first to sing for their suppers and then to pay the supper check. The creative folk now stood lavish hosts in their penthouses and country homes, at "21" or the Colony: it was the Joneses who at times had trouble keeping up with *them*.

But what is culturally and sociologically more interest-ing than the creative folks' social position in the old sense is their *general status* in the new. These people are literally *nouveaux riches,* and the question that must be raised hereafter is to what degree are they—in the quite pejorative sense—parvenus as well? However much or little they may have salted away, they are people able to own ele-gant penthouses and town houses and country houses; cars and boats, paintings and antiques and jewels; to travel as often and as luxuriously as they wish; to send their chil-dren to swank schools and camps; to maintain large staffs of secretaries, governesses, librarians, decorators, psycho-analysts, not to mention cooks, butlers, gardeners and chauffeurs; they are even rich enough for recurrent divorce

and resplendent alimony. Of these people, a small proportion were born to money and a somewhat larger proportion to middle- or upper-middle-class comfort; the rest
come from the lower- or lower-middle-class, many of them
from immigrant stock. Some got rich fast, when young; some
gradually; some rather late. The whole thing is a superb
vindication of democracy, though one still might question
the effect of it all in terms of social culture. For never
before has so large a group of the clever, the creative, the
talented—who in their own professional fields set the tone
and the fashions—been so much in a position to set the tone
and the fashions of high social life as well. Now, instead
of just embellishing society here and there, they compose a
large, affluent, "cultivated" society themselves. In terms
of worldly living, of what they consider charm, beauty, sophistication, they have now the material resources to command exactly what they wish and the numbers and prestige
to affect hordes of other people. The scale of this group's
living may not be that of the really rich, but the manner
very nearly is. For now, rather than gracing other people's
salons, they maintain their own—often with a principal
object of exhibiting the very rich, as once the very rich
exhibited them. In the past, indeed, when the well-placed
visited the clever, they virtually demanded a whiff of Bohemia, or at least of something "picturesque." But today
when the well-placed go visiting the clever, they see the
butlers they themselves have dispensed with, they dine in
houses where their uncles once lived. It is going too far
to say that things have reversed themselves, that the erst-
while patron or salonnière lives rather simply, while those
they would once have lion-hunted live in great style; but
it is going, at least, in the right direction.

Whether or not the whole thing points any moral, it has
its value as theater and its interest as manners. What stands
out most vividly among the New Plutocrats is not that they
aren't used to being rich, but that they aren't even started
toward being cultured. Nor do I mean they lack the snob-
bish fine points or small points of social cultivation—the
right-fork or right-allusion kind of thing: I mean quite
simply that despite their creative gifts, they badly lack

cultivated instincts and even natural sensibilities. They have taken their tone from a Café Society which itself hasn't any. Always, in the past, where there has been any degree of intermingling—as, most noticeably, in England since early in the nineteenth century—it has been between an upper class and a professional upper-middle class—that world of the Stephens, Arnolds, Toynbees, Trevelyans, Garnetts, Huxleys, Darwins. And despite differences of birth and fortune, there has probably been very little in breeding: both groups share the public schools and the great universities, the government services and even Parliament; while a White's on the one hand is matched by an Athenaeum on the other. Such an intermingling of birth and intellect has had real virtue, has made the intellectual and artistic world less provincial, the upper-class world less philistine; there has been a valuable, positive transmission of culture on both sides. (And where a whole succession of lower-class artists, from Dickens to D. H. Lawrence, have penetrated into upper-class society, they have consistently done so with an appraising and protesting gaze; even when most dazzled they have remained critically very sharp-eyed.)

In America today there is also much community of background on both sides, in the sense that neither side has any proper background at all. We have a double plutocracy; everything that descends from the Newport of the Robber Barons and the Palm Beach of the Boom, together with everything that is trying to rise from Broadway, Hollywood, television and commercialized art. Our creative plutocrats learn fast, which is rather proof that they learn nothing, not even how bad is the taste of their mentors. That they are accidental upstarts doesn't matter and is nothing against them; what does matter is that they are never natural arbiters. It is arid and dull enough to borrow, for most of one's life, the conventional good taste of others, but how much sadder to keep borrowing taste that is bad, to give up being oneself to become not an aristocrat but a vulgarian. To be sure, these people get well beyond the classical gold-garter stage: indeed, next only to watching them go fancy is watching them turn plain. They

soon reach that colorless, cowardly stage where they bid
you take pot luck in their $100,000 kitchen, a place ram-
pant with gadgets—gadgets in the ceiling, gadgets in the
soup. Nothing in their houses ever belonged to their families, or even to themselves twenty years before. It may
be argued that they come from poor and uncultivated
families; but whatever they came from, they came from a
home. They live in homes no longer; they live in stage
sets. They are dressed by stage dressmakers; they wear
sunglasses indoors; they sleep in twin beds with one back,
despite the prevalence of "modern" in their houses, there
is a curious effeminacy to the way the houses look; and
the more they mix styles, the clearer it becomes that they
were deliberately mixed as new pieces, that the whole thing
is not an accretion but a production. Their household
arrangements seem based not on what to get but on what
to get rid of, and one has a feeling that they somehow
trade in their living rooms the way they do their cars.
You feel that, even by accident, they couldn't be dowdy;
eating off their peasant ware, you half crave the blatant
declarativeness of solid-gold plate; while the twin-beds-
with-but-a-single-back evoke two minds with but a single
thought—and it is not necessarily sex.

To the old question whether money doesn't corrupt an
artist's talent and character must now be added another:
whether it doesn't actually vitiate his taste. It may even
be said to make it over, for it fails to survive in any recog-
nizable form. In a sense it ceases to be, since it is always
changing; it becomes not taste at all but submission to
the fashions, the peculiar fashions of people whose sense of
the gaudy must be always tempered by their sense of guilt.
It is not just an age of streamlining and functionalism that
leads them to contrive $100,000 kitchens rather than
drawing rooms; it is partly a faint sense of guilt, a social-
mindedness that jabs at their social success. But what survives, what will not down, is as much a matter of *social*
origins as what has been acquired: there is very little that
is *personally* expressive. In their flight from ostentation, the
New Plutocracy progress toward a philistine "good taste,"
a dead modishness; they are social hacks quite as often as
they are artistic ones.

THREE

1. The Matter of Being Interesting

IN spite, or maybe because, of all that has been written on how to acquire friends, exude personality and dazzle dinner parties, America today boasts pathetically few interesting people. By interesting one means, of course, quite the reverse of "interesting"—quite the reverse of travelers who give memorably minute accounts of their trips to the interior of Kenya; or people who have the ear, or hold the hand, or scratch the back, of the great and celebrated. One means people—it seems sad to have to say what one means—who because of their brains, charm, liveliness, responsiveness, wit are a pleasure to be with. And a pleasure whether one chooses to talk sense or nonsense, since the test of interesting people is that subject matter doesn't matter.

So few are such people that American life is chiefly conducted on the principle that human beings are dull. In general, American social life constitutes an evasion of talking to people. Most Americans don't, in any vital sense, get together; they only do things together. They meet by day to shop, play golf or tennis or canasta or bridge, go to football or baseball games, to matinees and movies. By night they gather—whether before or after feeding—to play cards or look at television, or they go to night games or movies or shows, or night clubs and bars. Though the servant problem has had something to do with the growing custom of dining out, people also dine out so that they can dance as well, or listen to music, or stare at the people around them. Such conversation as occurs tends to narrow down in subject matter and flatten out in style. Americans generally—Americans of all income groups—aren't interested in any great number of subjects, nor very bright or vivacious about such as they are. There are the people (and they make up the vast majority) whose chief delight, whose only alternative to bridge or baseball, the office or the household, is gossip. There are, again, the people (and they are rather more numerous than one might suppose) whose passion is for the "worth-while." The sad thing is that the first group can't make their gossiping sprightly, nor the second their earnestness stimulating. Gossip *is*, of course, the very life of conversation—if by gossip one means the all-too-human side of people, and if by people one means Einstein or Shelley as well as the members of the country club. Gossip—however intolerable when pursued with the sheer malice of the rocking-chair brigade—is the very watering can of conversation when indulged in with any tact. But just because it can be so spiteful, it needs to be handled with a certain real lightness, a certain sense of something left unsaid: the test, I would think, is that someone who gossips well has a reputation for being good company or even a wit, never for being a gossip.

Immemorial target for satire though it is, the pursuit of the worth-while must yet be touched on, since the plain sad point is that it can't possibly be laughed out of existence. There is no need to go after it at its worst, among women's-club discussion groups, or people with social-worker minds. But very near of kin to them, particularly in social life, are people who are both informed and intelligent, who may well possess opinions both sound and their own. Nor need such people, in order to strangle enjoyment, be opinionated or dogmatic: they may be really estimable people to meet, they may provide a stimulating exchange of views and meeting of minds. But that is all one *does* meet; as people they are ciphers, they lack temperament, they lack personality, they lack grace: *they* are not interesting. Even while they are flooding the conversation with light, they are draining it of color; even where they help restore one's faith in human nature, they help kill one's taste for social intercourse. And most of the time they are by no means so lacking in ego or assertiveness as I have permitted them to be; they all too often crush conversation by their need to hold the floor, or spoil it by their ability to suggest the classroom.

Middle-class social life, rampant with conformity, breeds the fewest interesting people of all. Here those who get the name for being interesting are, on the one hand, the life-of-the-party type or, on the other, the moderately eccentric or droll. Owing to the kind offices of such people, gossip soars into satire through giving imitations of their friends, through a certain amount of smug joking about their own bourgeois prejudices and of smugger joking about the would-be highbrows in their set. There are at times what might be called quite promising people in these two categories, but they either weary of such stuffy surroundings and hence flee the group, or they batten on its adulation and gradually come down to its level. And these are the better examples of their type: most middle-class people who are considered the life of the party simply possess a bottomless supply of radio gags and shady jokes, and a joshing manner, sometimes at the expense but always toward the entertainment of the group.

As for the group itself, it has no desire to be interesting; it thrives, rather, off being integrated, off having all its members interested in the same things, exhilarated by the same pastimes, fortified by the same prejudices. And for dinner parties and gatherings where outsiders must be conversed with, there is always "Do you know . . . ?"; there are all the season's hits to run through, and all the problems that agitate one's mind — servants, schools, pediatricians, bulbs and seedlings, rinses and permanents, point counts and forcing bids. For most businessmen the time spent at table where all the guests aren't known quantities constitutes rather a trial than a pleasure. Or it would were they not fortified with from three to five cocktails, and could they not brag or advise or flirt a little, or did they not just grunt and nod and steadily eat. But once the women take leave of the men at the dinner table it is usually for the rest of the evening. A man's bridge game is preferred to a mixed one; and when there aren't card games, or there hasn't been enough drinking or desire for soppy flirtation, the men gather for their brand of conversation at one end of the room, the women for theirs at the other. Nor is this sexual segregation limited to middle-class get-togethers; it has become *de rigueur* in many highbrow circles. The sole difference is that one group huddles to talk bonds, the other to assess Baudelaire.*

I don't think for a moment that businessmen are the Babbitts or philistines they once were; they have most of them had the benefit of college educations; they know something of the theoretical side of politics and economics, something of the practical side of medicine and law. Most of all, even while acquiescing in the pace and pressure of American life, they are "in favor of" leisure; indeed they ordain a certain amount of it for themselves. Every year or so they take a trip to Europe or Mexico, or go on a long cruise; they spend week ends, even "long week ends," in the country; every so often, just for the hell of it, they knock off for the day. And this in addition to the widened horizons I have spoken of elsewhere, to their being all too frequently moved around in business, or periodically sent to conferences and conventions. Contempt for culture is quite the wrong note for them to sound, though a kind of wry, self-depreciatory indifference toward the artistic or highbrow is still usual and proper. But the ordinary businessman of today is no more truly interesting than the businessman of thirty years ago; he is merely more presentable. In look, manner, surface cultivation he has come to seem much like the professional man; and indeed, between the fairly well educated and reasonably responsive business executive and the ordinary doctor or engineer

---

* There is a kind of cultural symbolism in many small acts of American living —for example, in the way two married couples dispose themselves when driving in one car. If they are working-class, the wives—one in the front, one in the back —sit next to their husbands: there is a sort of My Woman or avoidance of sexual temptation involved. If the couples are middle-class, the men generally sit in front and the women in back—a matter of common interests and conversational ease. (I've even seen a car arrive to pick up the second couple, with the wife already sitting in the back seat.) It is only at an upper-class or rather worldly level that each husband sits next to the other man's wife.

there is—special knowledge aside—little to choose. The best of our professional men are among the best men we have, but the bulk of them are as much in business, as blunted and dulled by the ways of business, as keen and alert for the rewards of business, as any broker or shirt manufacturer.

Actually, this more presentable type of businessman has helped *reduce* the number of interesting people in America. For, after all, a certain crudity makes people interesting just as much as a certain cultivation: in many ways, the next best thing to what Harvard represents is what the school of hard knocks does. Let no one sentimentalize the self-made man; he is frequently unbearable. But where he possesses any natural charm, or boasts any real "story," he can be extraordinarily much worth talking to. All too many well-placed men under fifty today, however, are the product of colleges and business-administration schools, much less self-made than machine-made. The traditionally self-made man at least had none of the earmarks of the junior executive or the field representative: he had the office boy's, which is to say the valet's, knowledge of character; he rather piquantly mingled a humble sense of his own limitations with a robust sense of his own worth. The new style of self-made tycoon either skyrockets to a seat among the mighty, in which case he is so big a fish it fails to matter whether or not he's out of water, or his economic self is so far ahead of his social self that he seems less a fish out of water than a bull in a china shop. On the other hand the older type of self-made man, smacking of the sand lot or the cornfield, kept the tang of where he came from along with the personal traits that made him rise above it: indeed, he could be most interesting of all for his very limitations and intolerances, for his not knowing or caring enough to view life along fashionably accepted lines. Nor do I mean interesting in terms of being a "character." He *had* character, and might often, too, have style; and it was because he could effortlessly command attention, and be as charming as he could be brutal, and as blunt as he could be poker-faced, that he was genuinely interesting.

Yet perhaps even he possessed more color and shock-value than authentic individual force, and hence possessed more fascination than interest. Some distinction between the two things would seem called for today, when so much in art, in literature, in life itself—so much that is peculiarly of the age—has fascination without interest. Fascination, I would imagine, has something a little unusual, enigmatic, even monstrous about it; it exhibits an element somewhat remote from our own make-up, our own experience, our own personal values—whether of the evil and criminal, the inscrutable and stealthy, the exotic, the mystical, the mad. It is certainly a primary characteristic of modern art and literature, whether self-consciously in a Dali, organically in a Faulkner, didactically in a Sartre or strategically—so to speak—in a Gide. Thomas Mann has contrasted Tolstoy and Dostoevsky in terms of health and sickness and of the classic and romantic; and though I don't think the distinction between interest and fascination is relatively as clear-cut, it is of no very different sort.* If there's not something of the pathological about the fascinating, there is at least always a touch of the sensational and strange.

The fascinating necessarily tends to call a certain attention to itself; the interesting need not. An evening spent with a fascinating person leaves vivid memories; one spent with interesting people has merely a sort of bouquet. One conceivable test of talk with a really interesting person is that you can't remember a single thing he said. I have already been didactic past my bedtime, and I won't try further to define what makes a man interesting, or to what extent it is inborn and to what extent acquired; but I doubt whether it can be acquired through anything you send for, enroll in or read up on.

But I would stress that an interesting person is far more than the reverse of a bore. There are plenty of people lively or intelligent enough to be agreeable company, or individual enough to have, as it were, documentary interest, or who have a flibbertigibbet charm that keeps them from being dull, or are so high-powered or down-right appalling as to make "bore" the very last word that would apply to them. Yet all these people, the likable no less than the

* Because our approach to art is so clinical today doesn't prove that our strongest impulses aren't peculiarly romantic; while the fact that romanticism is currently out of favor proves it even less.

offensive, do, I think, fail to interest us in the end: they remain pleasant to be with, but that is something else. The really interesting human being, like the really interesting writer, combines something personal with something artistic: both not only have manner enough to carry off what they do, but have an instinct about what is worth doing, and in just what degree, and with just how much gusto; and they never speak one's language so well as by not speaking at all. Plainly, the whole basis of sound social intercourse is knowing when not to finish a sentence. But of course such procedure penalizes people who are well informed, people who tend professionally to debate, discuss, diagnose, analyze, instruct and advise; and since most intellectuals today earn both their livings and their reputations by doing several of these things, most intellectuals today are not, in the perhaps peculiar sense that I use the word, interesting.

And if these people—so often provocative and informative and even wise—fail to be interesting, how much less must those who, by way of Dale Carnegie or the Five Foot Shelf, so strenuously seek to be. Yet there may be, for all that, a long-term ray of hope for the disciples of the Mr. Carnegies which is quite lacking for the assured and ambassadorial people one meets at dinner—I say ambassadorial, since they seem accredited to represent Sociology or Anthropology the way another man represents Sweden or Brazil. At least the Carnegie enrollers go on the assumption that they *aren't* interesting. I don't think that's a very sound basis for becoming so; yet possibly as much is to be hoped for from those who don't know what to say as from those who don't know what not to. And environment, which is to say example, counts for a good deal where being interesting is concerned. When, a couple of centuries ago, the cultivated classes obligated themselves to write one another longish letters at regular intervals, a fantastic number of such people wrote extremely good ones. When the cultivated classes were supposed to be gay and amusing at dinner, a large number of people were. It was much of a piece with learning how to play tennis or ride a horse; it carries us back to a world in which people were "accomplished." I don't want that world back;

the accomplishments came too high. But in terms of being interesting, or giving intelligent pleasure, there is something to be said for putting oneself to school a little, if not Mr. Carnegie's, then where one might learn how to be light on one's mental toes and to speak the sort of nonsense and banter that almost no one, nowadays, can even write for the stage; or how to manage irony, so popular in our time as a subject for discussion, so rare as a form of speech.

The whole matter involves the difference between the salon at its brightest and the schoolroom at its worst, the difference between holding the table and holding the floor. I don't know that on any basis of self-interest one need any longer go to much trouble, because, plainly, being interesting is no longer enough. It is better, and I dare say no harder, to be impressive. And besides, this is no age when people fold their legs; this is an age when people are on the run; when, no longer even furtively, they are always glancing at their wrist watches; when business keeps them rushing from one place to another; and they escape boredom by staying nowhere long enough to be bored. I would guess that the few people who are interesting in society less and less form any part of it. After all, they are among the few people left who are also not bored with themselves.

2. The American Sense of Humor

THERE is perhaps nothing we Americans feel more certain of than our sense of humor. In partial proof we can point to a vital humorous tradition and to a long, still-flourishing line of humorists. For the rest, it is indisputable that we have a famous method of joking. That method—very logical in a young, expansive, bumptious people—has been one of overstatement and exaggeration, of the tall tale and the woolly yarn, of bringing to our jests something of that giantism that has molded our dreams: we even joke, as it were, in six figures. Ours has been, almost entirely, a humor of release rather than reflectiveness, a fizz rather than a *fine*. There is little that is wise, there is little that is melancholy, about American humor—little, even, that can be called rueful. Possibly the best thing about it is the disbelief that gets hitched on behind the bragging, the "Sez you" that is tossed after the "And I said to him." But the snorting has much the same crudity as the boastfulness. We meet the braggart too much on his own terms: for though a world of humor can be insinuated into a mock bow, not much is possible to a Bronx cheer. Nor is the breezy manner at all a mask of seriousness. It's precisely because we are not, in the best sense, a serious people that we have ceased, in the best sense, to be a humorous one. At our worst, we have made our humor the handle of our acquisitiveness, a trick way of getting our foot in the door. Not only do we precede the moment of sale with the one about the two Irishmen, but signing on the dotted line is itself a quip.

It is because there is no longer a deeply self-critical quality in our humor that it is so much less cathartic. Our humor has become a confederate of our faults rather than their prosecutor. This has partly to do with our being such cocks of the walk, such top dogs in the struggle of life. The underprivileged, the downtrodden, the disreputable crack jokes that tell consciously against themselves

101

or that make a sad fun of their betters. "If this is how Her Majesty treats her prisoners," said Oscar Wilde, standing handcuffed in the pouring rain, "she doesn't deserve to have any." With such humor there will often go a certain self-pity as well, or a certain twisted contempt—the sharper's contempt for the sucker, the rogue's for the gull. But the humor of such people, even where it is cruel, is the badge of their humanity, of what makes them despise, equally, their victim and themselves. Such people have usually suffered enough, sinned enough, faced the truth about themselves enough, to *feel* the joke. In most good jokes about crooks, about failures, about trades or races or groups that are looked down on or discriminated against, there is an element to be shared, as it were, between *professionals*: they share and react to the joke as two artisans share and react to a piece of technical skill. Americans, in this sense, seldom "experience" a joke; they merely get the point of it.* Their jokes have become a kind of surface communication—the latest gag is a way out of having to find something to talk about, or a mere preamble to getting down to business. The breezy approach enables one, without changing the tone of one's voice, to change the basis of one's talk. Our national joke is the one about the traveling salesman and the farmer's obligingly innocent daughter —and fittingly so, since that is our dream *business* relationship as well as sexual one.

Yet even here we have covered up our tracks, transposed our symbol; for the difference between us and more serious or self-accepting races is that where their jokes are a way of acknowledging their true motives, ours are frequently a way of trying to conceal them. We try to suggest that there is a strong playful element in all our business dealings, but increasingly, I think, there is a certain self-seeking in all our playfulness. We "entertain" clients; we hand over tricky contracts with a "better have a damn smart lawyer give *this* the once-over"; we crack wise to take advantage of an employee—"Gotta chain you to the galleys tonight"; we make gags as a way of minimizing resentment. Originally much of this sprang from something genuinely

---

* Which is not unrelated to our already obsessive and yet increasing enjoyment of the gag—a form of humor that for the most part has point *without* substance.

friendly and democratic in American life, but more and more—and all the more for having the appearance of real humor—it is becoming a device.

We possess a certain natural good humor, but no great sense of humor about ourselves, no very rueful appreciation of our plights. We are not at all an ironic people, so that once our humor loses its disinterestedness it tends to becomes cynical and hard-boiled, a sort of cold chuckle. Our breezy averageness robs us, moreover, of stance and style. No American, faced with the proofs of his grand-scale buccaneering, would confess himself like Clive, "amazed at my own moderation." Our modern sports-jacket approach to the world—so youthful, playful, *un*-businesslike—is a touch misleading. To begin with, though it seems to break with a stuffy, over-solemn tradition, it is much more the product of an *arriviste* business class that never knew any such tradition and that, finding shirt sleeves comfortable, have gone on to make them respectable.

As for our brand of humor, the tall tale of the nineteenth century, being the expression of a young, healthy, hell-raising frontier people, gave something new and exhilarating to the humor of the world. Our contributions in the twentieth century—the gag, the wisecrack, the comeback, the nifty, the clincher—are nowhere so good. As long as it was expertly used—indeed, scrupulously stylized —in old vaudeville routines; as long, too, as it represented a second stage of American humor, a kind of retort on the tall tale's boastfulness, the American gag had its real virtues. But we have turned the gag into a mechanical, ubiquitous, incessant national tool so brassy as to be vulgar, so unchanging as to be dull. As for the comeback, though fond of it, we have never been very good at it; in terms of cussing and repartee alike, our truck drivers are mere duffers by comparison with even the average cockney. After all, the essence of a good comeback is a certain delayed sting, a certain perfection of surface politeness. Two Frenchmen who had been brilliant and bitterly hostile rivals at school went on to become a famous general and a distinguished cardinal. The cardinal, seeing the general, after many years, on a railway platform, approached him

haughtily and said, "Mr. Stationmaster, when does the
next train leave for Bordeaux?" The general paused, smiled,
said, "At half past two, madame." By comparison, how
very American at bottom is the most famous of modern
comebacks; how lacking in all subtlety and in any final
wit is Whistler's "You will, Oscar, you will."

There is a reason, I think, why our comebacks are so
crudely, so overtly abusive. The comeback flowers best in
a class-ridden society where people must preserve at least
the *form* of knowing their place and are thus driven in
their retorts into understatement, or double meanings, or
irony. Or it flowers in a cultivated formal society, where
the urbanity of the language is wholly at variance with the
brutality of the sentiment. In a democracy, where one is
free to speak one's mind, one is prevented, as it were, from
being insolent. We heckle rather than insinuate, and we
borrow forms of abuse rather than invent them. We have
even a sort of defensive guile about our lack of polish
and sublety in these matters. "An epigram," Oscar Levant
once said, "is a wisecrack that has played Carnegie Hall."
But it is not, and in his heart Mr. Levant must be quite
aware that it is not.

That our humor isn't deep or cleansing would seem be-
lied by a great many things—though it is perhaps just those
things that bear out my contention. We are humor-conscious
much as we are culture-conscious; we are extremely worried that we won't seem to show sense of humor enough
(particularly as a "sense of humor" has become a synonym
for being a good sport). We joke incessantly—but partly
from having reduced an attitude to a mere habit, and
partly because, conversationally, we have so little to say.
We shop for humor, we constantly listen to humor—on
radio and TV, at movies and shows; but that is from lacking more serious cultural interests and from being so bored
with ourselves when left alone. We have, generally, a
brisk manner; we many of us lead bustling lives; we are
still a "youthful" and often boisterous, slangy, sassy nation;
and all this would seem to make us notably humorous.
But a moment's reflection (a rare American trait) would
suggest that humor is not a matter of being brisk, but of
being reflective.

And though we once were open and hearty, were we ever—at any significant level—deeply humorous? In fact, could we have been? I say this rather to characterize than disparage us: humor, for one thing, isn't all pure gain; and for another, though purgative and health-giving, it often bulks largest in people who themselves are not healthy. Humor must largely constitute an appreciation, even an airing, of one's own and one's community's and one's country's faults, rather than a tribute to their virtues; or if that comes too close to defining satire, then humor is a gay confession and a wry acceptance of what makes us fools and sinners, goatish as well as godlike. Humor simultaneously wounds and heals, indicts and pardons, diminishes and enlarges; it constitutes inner growth at the expense of outer gain, and those who possess and honestly practice it make themselves more through a willingness to make themselves less.

Perhaps no young race can, in the very best sense, *be* humorous, for the crueler, cruder, more boyish, prankish, exuberant forms of humor neither greatly express nor truly educate. And it has been our misfortune as we have grown older not to have had, in our personal lives, misfortune enough, not to have been compelled to reflect or made to suffer. Creatures of noise and hurry, of hope and assurance, we have not had the time, we have never felt the need, to think hard on our problems or to confess our weaknesses. We have kept certain dead donkeys in our stables so as not to have to flay the living ones—and certain standard "goats" as well. Our national jokes are the umpire, the Milquetoast, the henpecked husband, the interfering mother-in-law, longhairs and sissies (whom we don't accurately define), suckers for gold bricks (the fool, not the knave!) and not the city slicker but the hick. All the symbols of push, of philistinism, of sharp practice—the joiner, the yes-man, the salesman, the Chamber of Commerce—are satiric figures created by an enlightened minority and objects of laughter to but a relative few. We laugh at polish (that is to say, Harvard) rather than push, at highbrows sooner than louts. Our humor is largely at the expense of what it is safe and indeed quite proper to despise: of what we don't want to be, can afford not to be, can with impunity make fun of. Even corruption thrives as a joke at the expense of those who *can't* horn in on it. We don't make fun of ourselves—only of our minorities and failures, of those who don't conform or assert themselves or measure up. Our humor, where it is directed inward and not at mere "goats," is almost completely flattering. We kid ourselves for being such reckless spenders and sports, such suckers for a good-looking girl, such soft touches for a hard-luck story; or, worse, we jest about what is wrong in terms that would make it seem right— just overgrown "boys" at reunions and conventions; just "cards" for perpetrators of various cruelties. We are really apologists for ourselves, as opposed to races that, like Negroes and Italians, have humility, or, like the Spaniards and Scots, have pride. In any important context, we tend to fear and fight off humor: Adlai Stevenson's Presidential campaign was a real anomaly and one that the nation felt sure could backfire.

No doubt humor, in the personal sense, is a distillate of suffering and, in the poetic sense, of melancholy; and it is no coincidence that we so often find it among the have-not races. More fortunate races, given to contemplate their blessings and to wonder how much they truly bless, are more likely to become ironic than humorous. America, in the deep sense, has neither irony nor humor. It is, on the one hand, still too naive; on the other, too shallow; in its ambitions and aggressions it is too much consumed with self-importance. Americans don't habitually see the wry humor of their plight, the sad irony of their triumphs; they go right on affirming the values that, even at the beginning, they hardly so much chose as had foisted upon them. They are only saved morally in the degree that they are so genuinely and wistfully lost. They haven't the melancholy of humor, but are the more lost, and more melancholy, for lacking it.

If we lack profound humor for lacking this poetic sense of melancholy, we lack it too from having so largely ceased to be spectators of life. We are much more a part of the game itself, or of the crowd who themselves insist on being looked at. And we seem destined to become a less humorous people because our twin gospels of Belonging and of Getting Ahead foster a sense of self-importance. Says a character in Sholem Aleichem: "I was, with God's help, a poor man." Americans, far from savoring such remarks, would quite fail to grasp their meaning. Humor, to most Americans, is not an inward way of looking at life, but an outward, good-guy way of living it. Humor, to most Americans, means grinning rather than getting sore when somebody hits you with a snowball, or laughing at yourself when you lose out through carelessness or anger. Humor, in other words, is for most Americans a matter of conduct rather than character, of the proper reaction rather than the owned-up-to-motive, and is but another facet of conformity. It is also a tactic at the other fellow's expense —a way of side-stepping sensibility and shame rather than feeling them. We hope—indeed often expect—that the wronged person will laugh the thing off so that we can join in, that *his* "seeing the humor in it" will take us off the spot. Increasingly, our humor shows a vital lack of criticism and insight, fails to educate either the heart or the mind; it is chiefly a salve or poultice for easing tensions, preventing scenes and snarls. Humor, it seems to me, has become a kind of national front, as politeness is with the French.

And as our humor grows more tactical, so our satire grows concessive rather than corrective. Doubtless most races get a certain pleasure out of joshing their own weaknesses and (as with the British on the subject of their insularity) are really bragging where they would seem to be self-critical. Self-satire is necessarily ambiguous; it provides those who indulge in it with some of the relief of the confessional, and it goes far toward disarming other people. Yet it is seldom practiced as a calculated maneuver. But what appears to be happening in America seems at least partly calculated; it constitutes confession *in lieu of* contrition; it is almost a way of serving notice on people that we may misbehave. We announce that we are part of the rat race as we might announce that we are part of the general public; we dub ourselves bastards as fair warning that we may be expected to behave as such. A single word like *integrity* proves, I think, extremely enlightening. It became, some time back, the cliché word for whoever felt guilt about leading a double life or for selling out. Today it is the cliché word for making fun of that attitude of guilt; from being an all-too-facile form of lament, *integrity* has become an equally facile form of lampoon. The word no longer has any dignity. And at least one reason why it no longer has any is that the man who begins by suffering from divided aims soons hardens into satirizing (and, in reality, writing off) his own dilemma. I was told of a playwright who asked another playwright at the opening of a third playwright's dismally bad show whether he was going backstage to congratulate the author. When his friend said no, what on God's earth could he congratulate him for, the first man sniffed, "Hell, you guys with your integrity" and strode backstage.

We are often, I think, quite literally trying to make capital of our sense of humor, to turn it into a social sheath for an antisocial dagger. Indeed, a man who uses his sense of humor at the cost of his *decency,* who has grown callous enough to satirize so as not to feel guilt or shame, is in the truest sense decadent; his is no better, though it is doubtless different, than the cold amusement of the ruffian. And it seems to me that the American sense of humor is being thus perverted—though there is still a great deal that is healthy and benign about it. But we must take care that it doesn't become for us the form of outlet, the kind of compensation, that sentiment is among the Germans—that, in the very act of letting something flow, it doesn't let a great more dry up. Without wishing to make too much of such standard cracks as "I'm a hack" or "I'm a Simon Legree"—or of ignoring the element of guilt involved—it is yet true that this kind of thing has become so constant a tactic as to be by now a mere habit, a way of making things less culpable or monstrous by giving them not just the air but the actual status of a joke. The point about classic satire is not that in actual practice it necessarily proves corrective but that at least the satirist is himself disinterested, that it is not face-saving only. "I laugh," said Figaro, "in order that I need not weep." "I laugh," says part of America today, "in order that I need not blush."

3. The One and the Many

WE were never an artistic people, and we have ceased, on the whole, to be an individualistic one. Conformity is one of the first words applied to us by foreigners, one of the first that, in critical moods, we apply to ourselves. It is rather natural, that, coming very late on the scene, America should have accepted the standards and followed the fashions of others; or that when it later began creating standards and fashions of its own, it should have followed up any momentary audacities with a countervailing sense of caution. So long as American life was crude and primitive, there was doubtless enough "bad taste" displayed to create something nationally picturesque, enough indecorum to suggest individuality. While men still ate peas with their knife, danced in mud-splashed boots, went to bed in their underwear, spat like marksmen into cuspidors and swigged whisky royally out of the bottle, their very colorfulness set them apart. But theirs was the conduct, after all, of a whole frontier society. It constituted very strict conformity of a kind, so that we may wonder which of these men would have dared, in the company of others, to eat with a fork or spit into a handkerchief. But of course this type of conformity is not racial or national: in all frontier societies we find people frightened of putting on airs or of seeming like milksops or dudes; in matters like these there is much the same ritualism as governs underworld characters or schoolboys; and men are "refined" under pressure from their womenfolk—a pressure that usually refines them *en*

109

masse—or after they have moved on to a higher sphere of society.

Paradoxically, the strong American tendency to conform may have been fostered by our very variety of cultural backgrounds. A nation like ours, made up of diverse racial strains, each with its own mores and sanctions, must have found "assimilation" and "conformity" almost exact synonyms. In the cities, Italian or German or Jewish or Irish sections might linger on, or later be grafted on, with a culture and way of life of their own; but in most small communities, with their half-dozen German families, their two or three Scandinavians and Poles and Jews, the dominant tradition—at any rate, among the middle class—imposed itself rapidly. Being "different" soon became a stigma rather than a mere circumstance, and being like everyone else constituted an achievement rather than an absence of one.

It is obvious that the want of a common background, of a common cultural floor, has increased the need in America for broad social likenesses. Had we possessed that common floor, we might have been far more tolerant of all other individual differences. But it is the function of a melting pot to melt differences down; it is the aim of a "new" country to build traditions up; and for a callow people so constantly on the move, so hungrily on the march, there had to be a sense of agreement about fundamentals.

Perhaps it is because there is so little conservatism of *manner* in America (here we have neither powerful class boundaries nor much natural reserve) that, while displaying energy and initiative, America should yet be conforming to a basic philosophy, a recognized master plan—the gospel of getting ahead. In old and class-dominated societies the pattern of conformity, the rules for communal living, have been for the most part static. They have been ways of preserving the kind of world one was born into; they were concerned with holding onto something. In America, however, the pattern of conformity is peculiarly dynamic: it consists not in preserving the world one was born into but in acquiring and asserting the point of view (often a succession of points of view) of the world one aspires toward. There is conformity to a single idea, but since the idea itself is that of material advancement, one comes to imitate a whole series of attitudes; one grasps, as it were, the etiquette suited to each rung on the ladder, while no rung on the ladder is, ideally, the final goal.

Whether a large number of people scale the entire ladder is immaterial; what is important is the assumption that they will; and in fact the number who do scale it, or a very considerable part of it, is surprisingly large. And of course the very gospel of Getting Ahead imposes a special need for conforming: one almost has to conform because the pace one moves at, and the always new country one is moving through, leave one too insecure and ill-informed to strike out for oneself. The classic Success Story pattern compels one to vacate a given social milieu just when one may be supposed to have mastered its secrets. The Moving Van is a symbol of more than our restlessness; it is the most conclusive possible evidence of our progress.

Thus, though the whole impulse of American living is to conform and the whole aspiration is to belong, what one actually conforms to is less any given set of ideas than the gospel of conformity itself; while the essence of "belonging" is to pass *beyond* what one belongs to—to make being established the key to being advanced. American conformity, at bottom, is adaptability, a kind of endless When-in-Rome-ism. Americans, in the course of moving upward, must again and again wear different clothes, eat different food, belong to different fraternal orders and then country clubs and then city clubs, take on subtly different opinions about marriage and divorce, politics and art, sport and education; they must keep up with fewer and fewer people, but keep up more and more appearances. From having—to take one example—no connection with horses at all, they come first to bet on them, and then to ride them, and then to breed them, and then to ride them taking a salute, and then to ride them mallet in hand. At bottom it is no doubt a case of *Plus ça change;* but in everyday ways it is a case of delicate variations in ethics and etiquette. It is the essence of a classless society that it must in some sense be a formless one as well, where things tend to merge rather than be set apart. Doubtless there is a point beyond which one is definitely committed to the middle class; and another point, less easily defined, beyond which one is definitely committed to the upper middle class; and finally one which identifies one with the world of top executives. But part of being somebody in America consists in being about to turn into somebody else; so soon as one doesn't belong to the future, one begins to belong to the past.

There are accordingly no set ethical beliefs, no immutably established values; and all this might have real virtue in it, might have the openminded fluid look of progress. But actually, as one moves along, rather than have to conform to less and less, one must conform to more and more. It is enough at the outset to seem alert and ambitious, to show a surface respect for the proprieties, to go to church and be a family man and not get too drunk at the office Christmas party. But though already one's soul may not be quite one's own, one's time outside of office hours is; and though one may lack the means to do most of the things one would like, one is not yet forced to do too many things one doesn't. But in the late stages, at the high social levels, among the top income brackets, one must—in about equal proportion—both follow examples and set them; and since at this level one's slightest movement is news, and hence known, and hence a public act, it must be done with a great care for effect and an equal care for consequences. The outsider or the underling, as he watches the big shot perform, may imagine that his work were better called play; he is conferring with another big shot or advising still a third; he is rushing about in planes and private cars; is put on committees, awarded degrees, cited, quoted, delegated, appointed, elected; he is wined and dined, and wines and dines in turn; he moves from cocktail party to reception, from testimonal dinner to public banquet, from the Governor's Mansion to the White House, from Washington to London. But it is perhaps more accurate that his play should be called work, if only because it has become indistinguishable from it. Lunch is no pause in the day's occupation, but more likely one of its high points. Dinner is no way of blotting out the day's exertions, but rather a way of crowning them. By now the setting an example has become a sacred obligation; where earlier it was enough to obey the law, now it is required to expound and uphold and at length embody it.

We perhaps think of all this as largely restricted to political life, to kissing babies or chopping logs for the photographers. But to maintain the role of a great executive, of a real molder of opinion, one must seem always to display the Open Mind, to Give Ear to the expert, to "Meet With" the foreigner, to hear what the Other Side has to say. One must be Easy of Access, whether to employees or stockholders or (should they have followings) cranks. And this is to omit all the parleys having to do with business itself. The big shot, at least on an hours-per-day basis, is perhaps the greatest conformist of all, since he must adhere to the rules he lays down: he becomes the great booming clock by which all the others set their watches.

The prevailing formula offers Americans a great deal, as it were, in Navy terms of seeing the world and, in social terms, of leading a host of lives. A really successful American who started, classically, in a small way in a small town can look back at the age of sixty on a life very rich in physical activity and even in cultural experience. From an agreeably anonymous provincial boyhood, he will have gone to college, where he will have picked up new traits and ideas; and having gone from college to work, will, in course of becoming an executive, have known big-city life at various levels. He will have known, besides, the suburban life of the commuter, and now, at sixty, will know the seignorial life of the estate owner. He will have dabbled in resorts and beach clubs, in country and town clubs, and will have gone—and less and less as a mere tourist—often abroad. Such a man will certainly have great intelligence; and at sixty will certainly not be crude, and may well have great background and taste.

And yet though the pattern is neither rigid nor provincial, though in moving up one moves considerably about, though in the drive for power there is time for many forms of pleasure—for all that, the variety of American Plan success resembles the variety of the American Plan meal. What strikes one first is the amount of variety; what strikes one next is the amount of sameness. American success turns out to be a kind of variations on a single theme—or, rather, of vibrations on a theme by X. The worst aspect isn't that one theme inspires all the variations but that it is a theme of someone else's making: one can lead any number of lives, dashing and even dazzling; but not one's own. More, I think, than even the luxuriousness, it is the outward variety, the changes in pace and background, that make the success story so enticing for those who live it—and so misleading. The great corporations, which seem less and less like businesses and more and more like governments, don't so much carry their promising employees up a stairway as put them on a kind of spiral sight-seeing bus. The white hopes are shifted from department to department, even from continent to continent: from being in charge of sales in Rio they pass to being in charge of personnel in Rome; now they are assistants to the president of their corporation, now they are on loan to the president of their country; it is their job today to sit around and listen, tomorrow to go out and speak. It is a genuinely educative and broadening process, it inculcates, as it all too soon involves, the worldliness and sinuousness of a diplomat; nor does it demand that trait so generally assumed of diplomats, a profound sense of irony.

I have been so far painting a particularly imposing set of murals. I have been treating of the real opinion molders, the upper two per cent. The picture, even among most very successful Americans, isn't usually quite so spacious; but even in the regions of, say, the upper ten per cent the variety today is as considerable as the rewards. Where there was once a mere class of executives, there is now a whole race of them. The old bank vice-presidency lodge, which at no extra cost enhanced an employee's value by increasing his self-importance, has doubtless tinged the word *vice-president,* or even *executive,* with something ambiguous. But the fact remains that with the development of so many huge corporations, the breaking them up into so many subsidiaries, the interlocking of divisions and departments, there has grown up a real need for all sorts of executives, whether hirers and firers, okayers and yes-men, surrogates and designates, grand exalted rubber-stampers, masters of the mimeographed memo, advisers to advisers, idea men and what's-the-idea-men, licensed barflies and chartered clubmen, greeters, note takers, decoy ducks, gentlemen of the bedchamber, not to speak, of course, of super salesmen, publicists, company lawyers and members of the blood royal—all the sons, brothers, nephews, cousins and sons-in-law. The very fact that so much of American business is conducted in the guise of pleasure, that so many deals are consummated not only pen but highball in hand, that the fifth tee vies with the inner sanctum, the club lounge with the front office, the commuter's train with the customer's room: all this, judging by how you look at it, either confers social life on the businessman or condemns him to it. Bridge, poker, golf, tennis, sailing, fishing, bowling are as useful "accomplishments" as embroidering, japanning and French once were for young ladies. Furthermore, in any age of chain stores, branch offices and international affiliates, even the most modest type of manager can live in all kinds of places—in small city and large, town and suburb—and need be neither a big shot nor a buyer to go abroad.

Reasonably successful people get around much more than they once did; there is even a greater exchange of ideas and a far greater acquaintance with styles and customs. Your most commonplace junior executive will, likely as not, serve coffee he drank in New Orleans, a cocktail he was introduced to in a ship's bar, a casserole dish he bought in Italy filled with a stew he encountered in France. Such a man is enormously superior to his counterpart of a generation or more ago. He has, in fact, such new "racial" characteristics as to suggest the emergence of a new race; and his greater awareness of other cultures, his being himself (in a small way) the product of cross-cultivation, is what is interesting and often valuable about him. What is not so satisfactory is that the new characteristics are all such typical ones, that he is as much a current type as his predecessor was a type forty years ago. We have advanced —and it marks a real advance—from the sort of street where all the houses are architecturally alike to one where the houses are structurally one but show a diversity of façades. The weakness rests on its all being typical, on the fact that our budding big shot can find enough variations on the given themes to feel no need for anything truly individual. The best people in this category would be as able to appreciate Babbitt today as were the enlightened minority thirty-odd years ago. Their satirist, who is often equally their spokesman, is Mr. J. P. Marquand. Yet, less gauche, ignorant, provincial as such people are, the difference in the end represents rather a change in strategy than a change in substance. For all the evidence of free will, a fundamental determinism still prevails. It would sometimes seem that this new race was called into existence as a way of destroying individualism by making it seem superfluous. For what, after all, can any prospering adherent of this clan deeply long for? On his place in the country he can have not just his own swimming pool but his own Walden Pond; and to this Thoreauvian hideaway, armed with a pitcher of Martinis and reading matter after his own heart, he can repair for a few hours every week end, blotting out not only the business crises of the previous week but equally week-end guests and his own family. He can commune with nature, or reflect upon mankind, or simply fall asleep—but at any rate return refreshed. His country place, again, can have any Recognized Architectural Look; no food can seem too exotic or peasantlike, though (since he is a man of sense) his drinks will be on the conservative side. And in choice of guests, as of food, he can be, within reason, quite orthodox. He and his kind have pretty generally rejected stuffiness; and, if he has any dash about him, or sense of the occasion, or gift for launching things a little sassily, there is no social experiment that need seem too bold—a cocktail party in the morning, a tennis tournament at night. His home is indeed his castle—and very possibly a castle inspired by Frank Lloyd Wright.

Who could want more? Who could live less in the shadow of a drab Puritanism, submit less to the decrees of an oppressive Philistia? In his world, such diversions as ballet or classical music are no longer thought longhaired, any more than a variety of social reforms are thought Red. Social conformity in the old sense hardly so much as exists. Fences are still up; taboos still operate; fine lines of demarcation still are drawn. But if the fundamental design has not changed, each man today may color it—as a child may his coloring book—to suit himself. Least of all need Mrs. Grundy be quakingly deferred to: sex is acknowledged, liquor approved.

The point is that not just one or two but that half a dozen related attitudes are culturally current, attitudes that the new race can mix and blend, arrange and alternate, to suit itself. In ideology, as in dress, gray flannels and odd jackets are quite correct, and at times the choice of odd jacket, the cut and color of the flannels, will be far greater evidence of belonging than the business suit. Indeed, as it becomes less obligatory to conform in strict detail, it becomes more important to show a certain real savvy of one's own. The key slogan is no longer "playing the game"; it is "knowing the score." And of course the catch is that the score is always changing and that in the end one must spend not less time but more in order to be *au courant*.

It is in a sense because success has become identified with knowing the score, rather than with simply learning the rules, that there is ever less true individualism in America. The English, with their class differences and more conservative social habits, may appear extremely much alike—at any rate, class by class; actually they remain more individualistic simply for being more adaptable. The American's ingrained adaptability, his quick surrender to his surroundings, indicates a sort of fear of individualism. Nor is this just a matter of When-in-Rome-ism: to adapt oneself as a visitor is quite different and completely sound. And of course much so-called unconventionality means nothing: a true individualist never balks at conventions bred of a desire for maximum ease, for maximum lack of friction. When Dr. Johnson declared that it made things much simpler to know that a lord goes through a door ahead of a commoner, he was no more striking a blow against individualism than against equality: he was only interested in saving everybody time. It is almost a mark of the wrong, even the phony, kind of nonconformity to make a fuss in such situations. Your true individualist will make himself as quickly felt in a sonnet as in free verse, in a dinner jacket as in corduroys and a beard: Flaubert, the arch antibourgeois, quickly nailed "the philistine in overalls." The true individualist is very much, I think, like the true artist.

In their social roles, most real artists are simple, even commonplace, and quite lacking in mannerism, because their talent all goes into their work; there is no need, as there is with the artist *manqué,* for it to slop over into their lives. So with your true individualist, who will either come to the country-club dance or stay home; but if he comes, it will be because he wants to, and he won't sniff and sneer at it while he's there. A certain firmness bordering on rigidity, a marked sense of character, betrays the individualist; and there will usually be much that is plainly French or English or American, Breton or Cockney or Yankee, about him, a good deal that springs from his family background or his early years. With your fashionable rebel, on the other hand, everything springs from later environment. Your determined avant-gardist, your orthodox bohemian, can only cast off the bulk of an unwanted past by casting out something of himself as well. But from never surrendering *himself,* the true individualist is less apt to shed much of his background. He will seldom know, because he will seldom care, whether he is "conforming." Simply because it suits him best, he may continue to dine at six o'clock and to eat the same kind of dinner he had as a boy. True individualists tend to be quite unobservant; it is the snob, the would-be sophisticate, the frightened conformist, who keeps a fascinated or worried eye on what is in the wind. Where mere fashion is concerned, individualists are usually the last to lay the old aside, if indeed they ever lay it aside at all. Whom fashion bores will care as little about keeping up with the times as about keeping up with the Joneses.

The English are more individualistic than Americans because, though where they *are* enslaved they are totally so, they are enslaved, on the whole, by fewer things. There are certain things an Englishman will not do for the sublime reason that such things are not done. Such transgressions are the mark of a cad or bounder, or they are proof of one's not being a gentleman, or a gentleman's gentleman, or whatever one wishes to be taken for. The sight (to the rest of the world) of an Englishman shoveling a small meal onto the back of his fork and then pile-driving it into his mouth seems every bit as needless as it is revolting; to a well-brought-up Englishman any other form of feeding is unthinkable and always laughed off as sickeningly genteel. (The prevailing American custom of the transferred fork is, of course, truly genteel; but we are not reduced to a choice between two such equally fantastic methods of eating.) The English, in other words, are the slaves of Thou Shalt Not: they will never flout what long tradition specifically, however insanely, frowns on. On the other hand, where a sacred tradition doesn't enter in, they completely suit themselves: fanatical about the Ten Commandments, they are anarchists in all else. Thus, though a certain harmless kind of jacket will simply, for all time, be beyond the pale, anything not expressly forbidden, however glaringly inappropriate, will cause no qualms at all. I have seen Londoners, with perfect aplomb, walking the streets at midday in white ties and tailcoats;* and I wouldn't have been surprised had they been carrying muskets or bird cages into the bargain. And as with their outfits, so with their ideas. It's not only adherence to tradition that makes the English unadaptable; it's their being as set in personal ways as in those of class and race. There are moments when all Englishmen are exactly alike, and others when each one is like nobody else on earth.

Their assurance springs from a very accurate knowledge of just when they must carry on, or play the game, or not let Eton or Ealing or England down; it springs from a deep sense—according to the only laws they respect—of being clearly, indisputably in the right. To "adjust" in such circumstances would hence not just be difficult; it would be close to treasonable. The furled umbrella has become such a comfort to the hand that clutches it, such a banner to the man who carries it, that it is carried on brilliantly sunny days and in steadily rainless climes: that it may cause stares is as little to the point as that it serves no purpose.

But if Thou Shalt Not quite governs the Englishman, he is much less affected than the American by You Really

---

* Someone will probably explain to me that they had been to a levee; but that still leaves out of account their aplomb in walking the streets.

Must. The difference is a matter of motive: the Englishman wants to be recognized as a gentleman, or as some
other suitable species of human being; the American wants
to be considered a good guy.* Americans are almost as
fearful of being thought eccentric as the English of not
seeming like the genuine article. I once knew an Englishman who refused to go out on Easter Monday for fear of
being detected in London when all the right people would
be elsewhere; but when he went forth on less dangerous
occasions, his get-ups were such as no American would
wear to a dogfight.

One virtue of British Thou Shalt Not is that it merely
creates key points, rather than an entire pattern, of behavior. British taboos are curiously assorted and oftener arbi-
trary than logical; they correspond to the idioms rather
than the grammar of a language. And being prohibitions,
they are things to observe rather than imitate; in other
words, one is obeying the law, not following the fashions.
The penalty for disobeying is ostracism; that for not conforming (along American lines) is unpopularity. The difference is in some ways profound; the Englishman either
walks free or is sentenced to hang; the American has to
worry about all the forms of social punishment between
the two.

Plainly enough; American conformity springs in large
measure from the American love and readiness for change.
America is so inventive that its people have come not just
to follow the cultural fashions but to count—subconsciously at least—on there always being new fashions to
follow. And Americans are kept so busy buying all the
latest gadgets, inspecting all the latest novelties, sampling
all the latest forms of entertainment, that they have a real
need of bulletins and bylaws and conducted tours: if they
didn't run with the crowd, they would be in grave danger
of losing their way. Not that all these minor adventures
in living make American life terribly adventurous: the activities in a prosperous suburb of any large American city
must be in most respects as prejudice-ridden and unimag-
inative as in any community that comes to mind. By com-

---

* There seemed to be at least a trace of this in President Eisenhower's wearing
a Homburg rather than the traditional silk hat on Inauguration Day.

parison, a New England village—however full of kinks
and intolerances—will seem almost anarchically rich in
character; and even a Southern town boasts a touch of
feudal boldness along with its measure of feudal thinking.
Nor are the ways of prosperous Suburbia always a matter
of large symbolic conformities — Gentile, Republican,
Chamber of Commerce, the things that prove a man "all
right"; nor of the things that proves he rates—Protestant,
well-fixed, college bred. These latter requirements will at
times seem too much to ask for; we are by now a *faute-de-
mieux* democracy, where half the people who rate actually
lack some of the prime requirements for rating: and though
the usual "good" suburb is something better than a mere
melting pot, it comes much closer to being fruit punch than
any sort of vintage wine. Its frequent thinness of "background" thus makes foreground behavior unusually important.

The foreground, as a result, must largely be façade.
There can be much show of novelty, a vivid sense of the
personal touch, but true adventurousness is seldom allowed.
People simply indulge the same inclinations in different
forms; people simple voice the same opinions in different
language. People, moreover, advance in step, turn left
or right in squads. If you are too unorthodox for the
community, you move away or find friends elsewhere; and
equally if you are too rich. Otherwise, you fit into a world
where people live better at fifty than at forty, and at forty
than at thirty—but not better than one another. With few
exceptions their houses are much of a size, they keep the
same number of servants, send their children to much the
same schools, join much the same organizations, play
bridge and golf for much the same stakes, choose much
the same summer resorts, go in for much the same cultural
activities. Those who are of a like social and economic
class will, to be sure, break up into smaller groups: there
will be a decorous set—the "backbone" of the community;
there will be a gay set that drinks, gambles and at least
flirts with the other man's wife; there will be a set that
makes some show of "keeping up with things," if only at
a Hokinson level, and that has a nodding acquaintance
with the arts and a wading acquaintance with bohemian-

ism. Such a community likes to feel that it isn't too "sot"; it very much wants a few wags and characters in its midst, one or two highbrows and mild parlor radicals, and men— though not women—with a past. It wants its tidy symbols of the untidy ways of life; but it wants them to exist much like characters in artificial comedy—where all is appearance and nothing reality, where there are picturesque crises but no actual consequences. The eccentric, at the proper time, shall wear a proper dinner coat; the parlor radical be a last-minute Republican at the polls; the bohemians shall know good food from bad, particularly when they give dinner parties; and though the highbrow shall be trotted out for company, or appealed to in disputes, he shall never hold forth on Beethoven when the others are ready for bridge. Conformity may not always reign in the prosperous bourgeois suburb, but it ultimately always governs.

In the bigger cities, among the better-income groups, there exists a kind of halfway house between conformity and individualism—a kind of mild cosmopolitanism that at least saves people from being stodgy and provincial. This perhaps discourages individualism even more than conformity does, since what it produces has the character—or lack of it—of a chameleon. The usual such cosmopolite is all spectrum and no prevailing color, speaks any number of social languages and has no real native tongue. Of course if he moves in identical societies in New York, Paris, Rome—if he but says identical things in English, French and Italian; if all he knows is bankers and businessmen, luxury liners and Ritz hotels—he must then, despite his knowledge of the best place in every capital to buy good gloves or good cigars, be dismissed as a provincial in disguise. And if, at the other extreme, he is a genuinely distinguished *homme du monde,* as much at home in colleges as in clubs, in senates as in libraries, he is then—whether a Henry Adams in one generation or a Harold Nicolson in another — too exceptional to express anything widespread in society. But there is a garden-type cosmopolite that lies between the other two.

In New York, for example, one can be, if not a true individual, a kind of companion to individuals. New York abounds in creative people—writers, painters, composers, architects; in people with artistic "connections"; in intellectuals of every kind, whether philosophers or scientists, psychiatrists of half a dozen schools, professors in half a dozen universities. New York equally abounds in people with hobbies—basket weaving or old fire screens or bookplates; in foreigners come to study or teach, lecture or give recitals; in professional men—lawyers, doctors, publishers, engineers; in businessmen of every level of sophistication; in authorities on highways or housing or city planning; in politicians and publicists. Furthermore, what is important, New York abounds in hostesses—some of them distinguished, others absurd; some at the top, some puffing up the staircase—whose métier is the bringing all the forementioned together. And though, at the most exalted levels, one is part of a world of celebrities, there is an equal cosmopolitanism—or opportunity for it—lower down; there is even something better about it lower down. For at the topmost level there are too many lions to make for anything so varied as a zoo.

But this kind of life is clearly limited to, at most, a few large cities: in more provincial communities, one encounters something depressingly ardent, self-conscious and second-rate. Culture becomes organized into the Literary Club and the Arts Club and the Busy As Three B's Music Club, and the Child Psychology Guild and the Women's Club lunches and the University Club suppers. In such communities "many-sidedness" is entrusted, and confined, to women; it is a rare man who is interested in how his better half lives. Or at lower levels, where men do participate, many-sidedness has a different basis. It can be the crassest and most philistine kind of joining and "mixing"—lodges, alumni associations, business groups, civic committees. It can be, again, a kind of friendly bohemianism, a determination not to fall into ruts: one spends one evening with the Jewish family down the block, another with the Italian family round the corner, a third with a rug merchant who serves Turkish coffee. Often one doesn't go with these people because they deeply interest one, but rather as one reads certain books or visits certain countries, because it is "broadening" and is something to talk about afterward. The solution to the passing boredoms of bourgeois life will never for long be the charm of bohemian living or the picturesqueness of foreign ménages. Few are the resultant richer lives, though many the recipes for *Streuselkuchen* or *espresso*. This is actually a form of mere tourism, of stay-at-home traveling.

The larger-sized university town has a chance for something better. Here, town and gown can be really useful to each other; for in the usual such community there are few people to provide stimulation, while in the usual compact college world there is no one to answer back. College faculties produce a great many people who are to all appearances highly individualistic, but the average professor can be narrow-minded as well as absent-minded; and any faculty forced to find all its social life on the campus can't help becoming inbred. The situation in small academic communities must be truly difficult—quite unlike that in, say, New York, where Columbia professors often choose to live as far from the campus as possible and when they leave Columbia for the day become completely independent of it. For the Columbia professor the world is all before him, where to choose; but can as much be said for, say, a professor at Brown, with Providence his guide?

Ideally, such cities as Providence, which are state capitals as well as university towns, should provide a very good kind of life. Here is every chance to mingle, and almost every kind of man. Here one should get beyond what is dreary and stifling in middle-class living, beyond all notions of right and wrong sides of the railroad track, beyond having to pay undue honor to the symbols—country clubs, Chambers of Commerce, good-guyism — that dominate American life.

And yet what this tends to produce in the end—and there is even no assurance that it will produce *that*—is rather eclecticism than individualism, a kind of informal education through others rather than any true expression of oneself. It offers a desirable and a frequent change of diet, but not necessarily any genuine nourishment. We are not always aware, I suspect, of the difference between leading even a full life and being oneself; nothing is perhaps better than travel, except a true and deep and very personal sense of home. Without that sense, one is in danger of becoming a receptacle at the cost of being a person. Nor is oddity ever proof of individuality. I was once taken to eat at a New York lunch club of pedigreed bankers. After lunch, members sat about with their hats on: what one looked in vain for was an individualist with his hat off.

It is not easy, of course, to detect individualism, since the truer the individual the less will he be given to outward demonstrations of it. Individualism is rather like innocence; there must be something unconscious about it. To be sure, in a society where public opinion speaks in such powerful tones it becomes harder and harder to be quietly oneself and to do as one pleases. It becomes increasingly necessary to *display* character, to reveal strong-mindedness, to stand out against this and stand up against that; it becomes increasingly harder not to be thought stuffy or surly or cranky. Moreover, I suspect that people can more safely flout public opinion by refusing to climb on band wagons than refuse, among their own friends, to play ball or be good sports. Many more people will risk being thought sinners than saints, wastrels than prigs; and though the basis for most satire on human pose and pretension is people's wanting to be accounted more cultured or intellectual or artistic than they really are, in recent times the satire might more appositely have concerned their pretensions to being he-men, good guys and lowbrows. The he-man aspect stands somewhat apart from the other two and is new only in certain details: obviously, the male animal has always been concerned with asserting its masculinity. Also, the past thirty-five years has put a peculiar emphasis on sex, has been an era in which sex first became a touchstone of social emancipation and then a basis for personal insecurity. America had no sooner got rid of being ashamed about sex than it grew ashamed about the lack of it. Mrs. Grundy had scarcely been routed when Dr. Kinsey arrived; and if one didn't kiss and tell, one at least kissed and didn't rub off the lipstick.

The he-man aspect—born partly of man's wish to strut, partly of the liberation movement of the 20's, partly of our growing anxieties about sex—has more point to it than the desire of the educated classes to seem like regular guys,

and even lowbrows, at all cost, whether in their amuse-
ments, their speech habits or what might be termed their
posing-in-reverse. "No man," said Dr. Johnson, "is a
hypocrite in his pleasures"; but though the remark has a
fine Johnsonian ring to it, it is unsound. A great many
people are utter hypocrites in their pleasures: gush over
Wagner but get drowsy even at *Lohengrin,* pant over chamber music, palpitate over art exhibitions; but from the
brave smiles they wear, you might suppose they were having
a leg set instead of their senses ravished. And today, it
seems to me, the loftier pleasures breed hardly more hypocrites than the lowbrow ones. There are as many people
today who fake their fun because they want you to think
they are good fellows as because they want you to think
they have beautiful souls. They like buttermilk, but they
guzzle beer, like croquet but take up Kelly pool, have a
yen for Bryn Mawr girls but carry on with chorines.

Take, again, the matter of language. Undoubtedly, as
life has grown more informal, speech has grown more
colloquial and slangy. Still, there has been a simultaneous
increase in jargon, in medical, sociological, psychiatric and
scientific terms: this is the age when every coal heaver
speaks of "antibiotics" and—as poseurs-in-reverse—most
college professors say *ain't.* All this is a further sign of
our inartistic natures—and vivid evidence, too, of our fear
of seeming different. Almost everyone today swears more
than his father did, but the level of speech means nothing;
one can talk like a book as well or as badly as one talks
like a boilermaker; and clichés are clichés, whether too
hard to pronounce or too filthy to print. Obviously, the
loss in real communication among educated people who
go in for "She's a honey" and "He's a bastard" is immense;
and the loss is not one in elegance merely (which most
people would judge no loss at all) but in precision, in
recourse to irony, and—where people clash—in that urbanity that can increase stimulation yet lessen heat. Vernacular
abuse, today, badly lacks freshness and color; and when
alcohol (a *sine qua non* of good-guyism) goes arm in
arm with cliché profanity, good-guyism can paradoxically
turn into the worst kind of brawl. But even brawls are
"human"; the real sin is to act superior, and a whole special

vocabulary has arisen to stigmatize putting on intellectual airs: *high hat, upstage, snooty, fancy-schmantzy, Haavard, highbrow* and how many others. But these days putting on airs can really be no more than a refusal to put on other people's clothes, no more than a desperate insistence on being oneself.

Among highbrows there is an instinctive defiance of regulation good-guyism, but they have their own brand of flirtation with the lowbrow, their own distinct brand of conformity. And highbrows, where they do conform, are perhaps the worst prigs and fetishists of all. They will play tennis but not golf, poker but not bridge, watch movies but no television, relax over detective stories but not over crossword puzzles. We all know why: golf and bridge are symbols of everything bourgeois and often evoke unpleasant memories of a bourgeois past. But intrinsically the differences are trifling, are largely matters of taste and are frequently examples of the most unworthy snobbism. And much too much has been made of the idea that while middlebrow culture is awful, lowbrow is fine. To be sure, lowbrow is usually preferable to middlebrow, possesses something coarse, honest and vivid where middlebrow is slick, genteel and innately vulgar. But an enormous lot that is lowbrow is merely stupid or cheap; an enormous lot is simply a damn bore. Virginia Woolf's attack on middlebrow helped sanctify lowbrow in an unwise degree, to which Aldous Huxley's attack on modish lowbrowism is a valuable offset. To be sure, primitivism has a strong and recurrent appeal, and the serious artist himself will often be refreshed or inspired on encountering it. My point, in any case, is less the merits of lowbrow than its present excessive fashionableness among non-lowbrows.

As I have said, an American has a wide choice of conformities and the opportunity to mix and blend them. But he must stay within bounds, he must not seriously infringe the doctrine of good-guyism, must very seldom be thought a bastard and never be called a heel; and such terms as *bastard, heel* and *quitter* are blanket terms for every kind of spoilsport, fuss-raiser or refusal to go with the crowd. Depending on the particular situation, one must be "cooperative," "openminded," "community-minded"; be willing to "listen to reason," to "see the other fellow's point of view," to "act one's age" and, above everything else, "play ball."* And involved in all this is a genuine impulse to do right, to prove helpful, to make life pleasant. But the fine phrases all too often accompany an intolerance of minority feelings; and good-guyism and majority-rulism, beyond being hostile to individuality, are becoming, more and more, the bedchamber women of self-righteousness. Where such attitudes so strongly prevail, whoever subscribes to them can't help feeling self-assured. And to the regular guy who is so much fortified by public opinion, the irregular guy must seem more than merely odd or affected; he must seem downright willful and unco-operative. Moreover, the average American's objection to oddity and nonconformity is in large part genuine, for it springs from a real lack of identification, from a truly bewildered sense of "Who the hell can *want* to see an Italian movie instead of an American one?" or of "Who the hell could want to own an old prayer rug instead of a TV set?" or of "Who the hell could want to spend his vacation studying beetles instead of going to the seashore?" And when such freakish tastes happen, in addition, to clash with the conformist's own desires, the individualist becomes not just a wack that can be ignored, but a nuisance, or even a menace, that has to be dealt with. There arises a real objection, not just an unconscious resentment.

The American imagination has perhaps been stunted by a kind of paradox—by the fact that the whole basis of American living is a vivid dream. But it is a rigidly blueprinted dream, a series of set, established visions; and the average American has grown so accustomed to his own form of dreaming that he can comprehend no other. When one is pursuing an ideal at breakneck speed, how can one weigh the merits of other people's aspirations? In a sharply stratified society, those who acquiesce in their own way of life can thereafter turn their gaze outward, will have the time and the curiosity to grasp the nature of other

* From the national game we have indeed taken the master phrases of the age: "play ball," that key to popularity, which is really half the battle of getting ahead; and "know the score," that proof of savvy and alertness, which is the other half. Though of course—and the national game still prevails—to get anywhere a guy has to have something on the ball to begin with.

ways of living, other beliefs and ideals. It is the realist,
who studiously learns the strict value and use of things,
that can in time assess the value and use of things not his
own: the very ability to compare and distinguish fosters
understanding. But the idealist, all of whose values are
more or less theoretical, so many of whose acts are acts
of faith, is nurtured by, is committed to, a dream. The
materialistic idealism that governs American life, that on
the one hand makes a chariot of every grocery wagon, and
on the other a mere hitching post of every star, lets every
man lead a very enticing double life, a life of strive and
succeed alike, of go with the crowd and yet personally
follow the gleam. What other road should he seek, what
other will have a more exhilarating ascent, be more brightly
lighted or prettily landscaped or widely traveled? Individuality in America is getting to be less and less sought
after; hence it needn't even be proscribed. It is disappearing
through lack of demand.

Here the fact that there is a whole network of conformities in America, rather than just a single pattern, strongly
enters in. Americans by no means all do things alike; they
just don't do them differently from everyone else. There
are cliques as well as crowds, summer rules as well as
winter ones, group revolts no less than group conformities.
Furthermore, the truly grown-up problem isn't how to be
oneself *out* of society, isn't Walden Pond as against Boston,
but how to remain oneself inside it. One of the saddest
things about conformity is the ghastly sort of nonconformity
it breeds: the noisy protesting, the aggressive rebelliousness,
the rigid counterfetishism. The village atheist would have
come to exist even with *God* for a next-door neighbor, for
he is an offshoot not of religion but of society; the avant-
gardist, again, is the last man to cultivate quietly his avant-
garden. In terms of set culture and community prejudices,
Bohemia and Philistia are the same thing in reverse, like
photograph and negative. In Greenwich Village and Greenwich, Connecticut, there are probably an equal number of
things the inhabitants wouldn't be caught dead wearing,
or furnishing their houses with, or tolerating among their
friends, or subscribing to as beliefs; the two places are
even necessary to each other—the one to be shocked, the

other to be shocking; the one to stare, the other to be stared at—and each place will feel for the other an exactly equal contempt. There are always places where a coat and trousers that match are far worse form than where they don't.*

I suspect, too, that the American distaste for individualism is partly due to our past forms of moral nonconformity, to our early crop of militant puritans and cranks. In pioneer days it must have often seemed as though cantankerousness were next to godliness. Our fetish of the good guy may well owe something to our inherited fear of the Puritan; the backslapper may well be a retort upon the bluenose; it has perhaps required all of the American dream to blot out the Early American nightmare. And once dissent has become associated with disapproval of all normal pleasures, clearly the inducements of a conformist society will prove very great; and the accompanying good-guy psychology will in time prove quite decisive. Even now, to be sure, a sense of guilt pervades the professional classes, the intellectual and quasi-intellectual world, though this is a sense of guilt derived from Freud rather than Jonathan Edwards. Something remains, of course, of the old New England conscience—and with it, quite admirably, something of the old New England character. But in general we are today a people who much less fear God than hate themselves. Moreover, where our current guilts aren't Freudian, they seem rather Catholic than Protestant—rather the Catholic puritanism of Ireland than the Congregationalist puritanism of New England. What dominates, in any case, is much less guilt than self-righteousness, much less breast-beating than backslapping. Even the clergyman—whether priest, minister or rabbi—does well to prove a good mixer, the church or synagogue to stress its clubroom and recreation hall. America possesses a few, but only a few, truly august figures, whether real or symbolic; the others best flourish by blending authority with affability. In all of this there is a sound desire to avoid the pompous: nothing delights us more than to find that the President of our country, or of our college, or of our corporation, is

---

* I am speaking here of conformity as a thing in itself; in terms of basic tolerance and essential *Gemütlichkeit*, Bohemia is enormously superior.

really one of the boys. This seems to me a valuable trait, a real safeguard against Communist or Fascist blandishments; we want our leaders to display the human touch.

Our well-founded distaste for cranks has, however, rather blurred our ability to tell a crank from a mere eccentric, or even an eccentric from an individual. On a very rough-and-ready basis we might define an eccentric as a man who is a law unto himself, and a crank as one who, having determined what the law is, insists on laying it down to others. An eccentric* puts ice cream on steak simply because he likes it; should a crank do so, he would endow the act with moral grandeur and straightway denounce as sinners (or reactionaries) all who failed to follow suit. The crank, however, seldom deals in anything so agreeable as steak or ice cream; the crank prefers the glories of health bread or the splendors of soybeans. Cranks, at their most familiar, are a sort of peevish prophets, and it's not enough that they should be in the right; others must also be in the wrong. They are by definition obsessed, and, by connotation, obsessed with something odd. They mistake the part for the whole, the props for the play, the inconvenience for the efficacy; they are spoil-sport humanitarians, full of the sour milk of human kindness.†

The crank is for several reasons a fairly common figure in American life. To begin with, our reaction against cranks has helped breed more of them. A society that worships good-guyism brands the mere dissenter a misfit, and people who are shunned as square pegs will soon find something deeply immoral about round holes. A society, again, that runs to fads and crazes, that has a natural turn for the ingenious and inventive, will encourage some of its members to be cranks and will doom others. There must be, so to speak, lots of factory-damaged human products that, from being looked upon as rejects, come to crankhood rather than true creativity. Careerwise, there is frequently

---

* Many "eccentrics" are, or course, mere poseurs and publicity seekers. But many are real, and I speak here only of such.

† They can be useful, at moments even invaluable, goads; but they fail of love no less than of humor, and seem most ready to plow the earth where they can spoil the lawn. John the Baptist *requires* the wilderness, and even a man of the critical excellence of Mr. F. R. Leavis evokes the workhouse. After all the gush of the Janeites, Mr. and Mrs. Leavis are well worth hearing on Jane Austen; but they, in the end, misrepresent her no less. They are the sort of people who, in assessing champagne, would give no consideration to the fizz.

a missed-the-boat quality in cranks, a psychological origin for their moral obsessiveness; and their "flourishing" off failure is tied up with their having failed at the outset. The crank not only increasingly harangues his audience, but the audience increasingly yawns at, and even walks out on, the crank.*

Where a crank is either a moral crusader by nature or a man at war with his surroundings, an eccentric is neither given to crusading nor oppressed by the world. Perhaps a certain amount of enjoyment is essential to the eccentric— his life is satisfactory *because* it is pleasant—as a certain lack of enjoyment is essential to the crank. The great blessing of eccentricity is that, since it is a law unto itself, one isn't constantly torn between what is expedient on the one side and what is personally desirable on the other. Something of an anarchist (as your crank is something of a bigot), the eccentric will often display very unsound, or unsocial, habits and beliefs. But there is nothing self-righteous about his wrongheadedness; he doesn't drag God into keeping a pet leopard in his back yard, or Americanism into going in for rifle practice at 2:00 A.M.

True eccentrics, I would think, are fairly rare, for they must not only differ from other people but be quite indifferent to other people's ways: they must, in other words, be as well adjusted as they are odd. So soon as maladjustment enters in, they cease to be characters and turn into cases. On the other hand, many people who with a little encouragement might emerge as eccentrics are, from childhood on, judged—and hence turned into—misfits. Where their peculiarities are mocked, and certainly where they are penalized, the results can be very unhappy. In America, where even the slightest individualist must resist great pressure, the true eccentric is never free from it. In England there is a proud tradition of eccentricity: the English are far more given than we are to keeping strange pets, collecting strange objects, pursuing strange hobbies, adopting strange careers; even where they most conform, as in their

---

* Just as many eccentrics are poseurs, so many cranks are charlatans. The charlatan shrewdly exploits human weakness where the true crank rails against it; the charlatan, preaching some form of nudism or trial marriage, some "holy" brand of licentiousness or God-sent type of laxative, may end up a millionaire. But the true crank has only a chip on his shoulder or bee in his bonnet, not a card up his sleeve.

club life, they will behave toward one another with what, to other races, seems a wild and splendid strangeness. This is so true that England's—and sometimes New England's—eccentrics have often a great air about them, possess style rather than mere singularity. Consider how Julia Margaret Cameron would walk the two miles from her house to the railway station stirring a cup of tea as she went. In England and New England on the one hand, and in most of America on the other, there may be a quite opposite basis for eccentricity: in the one case, the law unto oneself born of social privilege; in the other, the self-made born of being left out of things. The English eccentric suggests a grande dame, the American a spinster.

The individualist is by no means an eccentric. He is for one thing aware of alternatives; he chooses—for the most part consciously—between the expedient and the self-satisfying; he refuses to play ball rather than doesn't know a game is in progress; and he will seldom seem freakish or even picturesque. Yet, more and more, the individualist is being looked on as an eccentric and perhaps even a crank; though this attitude is scarcely deliberate on the public's part, it yet subconsciously—or by force of repetition—constitutes a gimmick, a pressure to make people conform. The other method of diminishing individualism in America has been to foster and develop "personality." Though the difference between "personality" and individuality is vast, there exists a strong, however thoughtless, tendency to identify the one with the other. So greatly has conformity triumphed that, no matter how orthodox a man's opinions or conventional his behavior, if he happens to express or conduct himself with the slightest vividness or briskness, he is rated and touted a "person"—what might be supposed an individual! Actually, he may not even have an iota of real personality, may just possess a breezy, adaptable, quick-on-the-trigger manner that enables him to be the life of the party or the spark plug of the conference. In the same way, a woman with a gift for dinner-party chatter and a feminine, discreetly flirtatious air will be thought to have enormous personality.

And though such mere types must be written off, there yet *are* a great many Americans with true personality—with an easy charm, a distinctive way of doing and saying things, a regional tang, a surviving girlishness or small-boy quality. They have the appeal, at the very least, of not being like everyone else. But that, in the cliché sense, they are "real persons" is to be doubted. One may go a year without hearing them utter an original, not to say controversial, remark, or seeing them perform a striking, not to say truly unorthodox, act. The centrifugal and extrovert charm of personality is in many ways hostile to individualism, which more naturally manifests itself in withdrawal than in contact, in quiet dissent than in eager acquiescence. Personality and individuality are by no means mutually exclusive, nor is genuine personality necessarily engaging nor genuine individuality necessarily difficult. But the fact remains that we regard personality as a decided blessing, as something a man can't have too much of, and individuality as, oftener than not, a handicap. Individuality is almost by definition antisocial; and the sound "social" maneuver—or it were perhaps better called instinct—is to discredit individuality and eventually outlaw it through enabling people to live *colorfully* alike. As for "personality," it has passed from having great social to acquiring great economic importance: it is the prime mark, and prize asset, of the salesman. And ours is the country where, in order to sell your product, you don't so much point out its merits as you first work like hell to sell yourself.

Last Thoughts

ONE tends to take one's blessings for granted; and in a book like this, doubtless what seems wrong with American life is given an unfair prominence. But such a bias might be assumed: one does not wisely write a book to tell Americans how fine, or even how fortunate, they are. As a people, we go in for self-congratulation enough; and too many of our American blessings rest on a fortune-building rather than a character-building base. Where our blessings are truly notable, preserving them is far more important than proclaiming them.

Nevertheless, without relaxing one's strictures one may—and in fairness, indeed, one must—seek to balance the portrait. Most nations, like most individuals, have the defects of their virtues, and vice versa. The English, the Goncourts once said very shrewdly, are honest as individuals and dishonest as a nation. Quite naturally the English visualize and exhibit themselves as people who might see money on a table for fifty years without once being tempted to touch it: of the swindling and buccaneering by which they took title to large portions of the earth, of the cant and specious reasoning by which they have justified, and even glorified, such doings they are somewhat less acutely aware. Similarly, Americans have every right to be proud of a pioneer heritage that, first conquering and subduing the land, has gone on to harnessing and commandeering the air waves. Americans are right to exalt a national ideal and a native *modus operandi* that, beginning with maximum hardship, has ended in maximum comfort. Why shouldn't we be proud of how openhanded and hospitable we are, of how alive and alert, of how the American Way has conferred unimaginable opportunity on the poor and

the elsewhere rejected? Why shouldn't we take pride in
our ability of fight wars no less than to finance them? As
for the wicked dollar sign, if we do indeed set vast store
by it, if we do steadily woo and even bow down to it, how
freely and generously we give money away, succoring the
needs and even the longings of others. If, again, we spend
an appalling number of hours witnessing, analyzing, fore-
casting and second-guessing baseball, what a safe and de-
cent national sport: we are no Prussians brandishing sabers,
or Latins slaughtering bulls. We are, I think, natural and
incorrigible do-gooders; and what is particularly to our
credit, we get real pleasure out of making other people
happy.

The real trouble is possibly our having less a love of
making money than a genius for making it; apparently it
is the thing we do best, the thing that comes easiest to us;
and it appears to interest us as much for what it is as for
what it brings. For us, business *is* pleasure, as against,
say, the French, for whom it is business to the last cen-
time—after which, they seek pleasure unalloyed. We deplore the fact that Americans retire and have no cultural
strivings or inner reserves to take the place of business.
But in truth there is nothing they feel the same zest for:
it is almost a matter of temperament; and relaxation after
business is weak tea after wine.

The original Puritan strain may have a good deal to do
with our being, today, so overwhelmingly a business civilization. We are partly driven to hard work by our uneasy
feelings about pleasure; and since pleasure can so easily
be bracketed—and so immemorially has been—with vice
(whether drunkenness and debauchery or idleness and ex-
travagance), it is not too hard to hail business, under its
maiden name of hard work, as the seat of all the virtues.
That industry and forethought, sobriety and moderation
are the tutelary deities of money-making, the guardian
angels of the fiscal year, has been sufficiently satirized, no
doubt, but insufficiently stressed as part of our daily thinking. (We blithely ignore the element of cant involved, but
sharply emphasize the element of character-building.) A
man at his office—assuming the office itself is respectable—
is innocent till proved guilty, whereas a man anywhere else

during office hours is guilty till proved innocent; he is either putting second things first or playing some kind of hooky. The puritan, in America, is father to the philistine,* with the result in America that business *is* pleasure, not simply because of the joy we get from making money but also because of the sense of virtue it bestows—of serving the community, along with ourselves, in making it.

Moreover, the puritanism has slowly arrived at a compromise with the flesh and the Devil: a man, today—provided he works hard when he "should"—may, after hours, splurge or hit it up for all he is worth. So much so that after-hours pleasure is subject to few restraints, is identified with the most frivolous and sensual forms of amusement, is almost a matter of small-boy fun. The businessman, after hours, is a *tired* businessman, for whom amusement must be free of the smallest intellectual demands and rich in the most primitive physical appeal—a sort of sport by day and sex by night (and of course there is spectator sex at musicals and night clubs no less than spectator sports at ball parks and fight arenas). The businessman, when he goes on vacation, is commanded to relax: his mind is directed to turn into a blank; his powers of judgment, concentration and reasoning—save only at the bridge table—must be totally suspended. Day in, day out, he is to hit a ball on a links or vacantly await a fish, lie for hours on a beach or drive a car furiously from one hotel, or one motel, to another. If he picks up a book, it must be after lunch with the express idea of falling asleep over it. If he is truly American, and not a mere spoiled loafer or secret rebel, such forms of pleasure, enjoyment, relaxation, of whatever you call his three or four weeks of sun and spray, must begin to induce a certain restlessness, and then satiety, and then despondency: once the limbs cease to cry out for stretching, the brain will beg to be put again to use. Or, even as he lies prone upon the sand, or sits mindless and motionless in the dory, his brain—with a joyful sense of guilt—will dart cityward, to the deals, the conferences, the agenda ahead. And on the beach, or in the bar,

---

* By condemning pleasure and the nonutilitarian satisfaction of art as a danger to morals, he has tacitly fostered and sanctioned a strictly utilitarian and materialistic philosophy of life. (Ironically, of course, if in America business is pleasure, and pleasure is vice, business is vice.)

one businessman necessarily comes to know another and to talk business in the third person, as it were, as of something far off and concerning someone else. Often, however subconsciously, the Monday morning that means return to work will be awaited with more real impatience than was the Friday evening that spelled the start of leisure.

He comes back from his vacation with the proper coat of tan (which doesn't rule out an accompanying look of fatigue) and—if his vacation has been spent at the right place and in the right manner—with some business cards in his wallet, some new names in his address book, a couple of tentative lunch dates, and somebody's best regards for the Big Boss. There was no intention of talking, let alone transacting, business while away, and perhaps nothing will come of any talk there was. Business got into the conversation because there was no chance of keeping it out: after casting about for acquaintances in common, and talking sport, and post-morteming bridge hands, and swapping kids and schools, and college days, and political gags, and dirty jokes—where else could talk tend?

The business of getting on in America is in itself a kind of art and culture, a real substitute for other "pursuits." The trouble is not that one serves God and Mammon both, for one often very understandably must; and perhaps one's salvation even lies in the knowledge that one must, since on the basis of it one may set about serving God as often, and Mammon as seldom, as possible. The trouble is not even, in the end, that one serves God and Mammon both, and both at the same time—with the result that things get marred, murky, impure. For such is the deplorable, but not disgraceful, destiny of man. The real trouble in this country is that more and more one sees God in the image of Mammon, one serves God as Mammon is served: as though he were some badly-pressed-for-time Big Boss, some celestial Chairman of the Board, referred to by his initials. It is as though G. A. would want his colleagues and assistants and aspirants to serve Him, not with all possible reverence but with all possible efficiency; and as though Heaven were no abode of harps and angels (could anything, really, be less fun, or less American?) but were rather a great corporate entity where one opened a staggeringly large Monday-morning mail, gazed on mammoth-sized Board Room charts and boasted a Recording Angel whose books the heavenly auditors would find 100-per-cent free from error. It is easy to miscomprehend (and dismiss) this as a vulgar idea of Heaven; but possibly Heaven is a vulgar idea in itself—a fervent assurance that virtue is *not* its own reward, that virtue pays. And so long as virtue does, why shouldn't the rewards be such things as one has always wished for and never had?

Thus what so plays the deuce with things in America today is not that we haven't idealism enough, but that we haven't enough sense of reality. Serving now God, now Mammon, and now the two at once, we haven't found a middle ground, we are literally mixing extremes. And we revel in the mixture, we exalt one extreme by way of the other, we justify our money-grubbing through what we grub for and how much we give away—just as we justify our oligarchical dreams from their not being aristocratic ones, and open to all comers. In so much of our business life we are both performing our duty and affirming our destiny; and in our daily living we keep something of the dream, as—throughout an entire lifetime—we keep something of the boy. We infuse sentimental elements and pious motives—home and mother, and getting the best there is for the kids—into our success stories; and though we rather admire cleverness, yet—even while trying to be clever—we are somehow suspicious of it; and we quite honestly save all our real praise for Character. We love goodness—and not as the evil and decadent do, with a twisted, excommunicate envy, but as something we understand, and wish to achieve, and feel sure we have in us. For all his connivings, for all his wrestling matches with conscience, the average American never sees himself as wicked or as permanently lost: he feels that he will turn good with age, exactly as that someday he will retire and see the world. We keep something of the boyhood dream, in part from never wholly surrendering our innocence, but in part as though there were no other, no later one. There is the one dream only, of God and Mammon blent. The dream may fade, but then we have it touched up; or fade at length into a blurred illegible memory, a relic for death-beds and high occasions; but no other dream replaces it.

We lack realism drastically, fatally. Very few of us actually know just what we want in life; very few of us ever weigh the precise value of things against the exact cost. We seldom examine the big crises in our lives—crises of character quite as much as of career—with any sense of putting a top price on them. If we only knew just how corrupt we were prepared to be, instead of always wondering how unblemished we might emerge, surely it would spare us our wild pendulum-swings between God and Devil, between heroic resistance and abject surrender. Though the thought may sound horrifying when put into words, the ability to live by standards that are partly second-rate not only makes people generally happier and saner, but it also promises more in the way of slowly raising one's standards than does the current inability to maintain any consistent standards at all. If one *has* to make deals, one should make them with oneself—vow to resist four bad impulses in exchange for giving in to the fifth.

As it is, we increasingly tend to rationalize our infirm positions—to let a kind of moral death-wish, a kind of capitulation-compulsion, eat into our idealism. And all this is quite as much the enemy of culture as it is of character. All this makes us degrade things in the very act of improving them—because the pure, benign element, the thing that causes the improvement, is itself—by contact with the rest—degraded. Thus we have introduced humor into our business dealings, as though it imparted something open-handed and Lincolnian into them—where in practice, business becomes only more fraudulent without ceasing to be cold-blooded, while our humor lacks what humor cannot be permitted to lack—disinterestedness. The radio commercial that spits on its product is profoundly vulgar, because far from being honest satire or healthy criticism, it is the merest gimmick to get people talking. (On the other hand, where advertising becomes human and genial, as with the Wallach ads in New York, the commercial motive may honestly boast a civilized manner.)

Again, informality in social relations is certainly desirable, but in removing the starch and the whalebone we often remove what is dignified as well as stuffy. Informality—as I remarked earlier—has become a barefaced tactic for invading people's privacy, for exploiting their acquaintance, for insisting that *they* behave like good fellows—on pain, should they not, of being branded heels. "Frankness," again, may have great value during an age of mealy-mouthed evasions and hypocrisies; frankness, today, is all too often simple presumption. The very act of liberation performed by psychiatrists today; the very fact, again, that so many of people's true motives and subconscious desires are common knowledge, has proved corrupting. Define evil as sickness, and along with giving it a proper claim on men's understanding and compassion you offer it a tactic it can viciously exploit. It can now (as once it could not) cry your pardon—even make *you* a kind of villain for not granting it. And such crying out has become a widespread practice: people today turn their personal failings into Contemporary Phenomena; they identify what is ill-behaved in them with the *Zeitgeist;* they become stock-holders in neurosis; they are magnificently realistic about the "age" and quite cavalier and irresponsible about themselves. They have created both new *styles* of behavior and new *standards;* and with a keen awareness of how much of life is pathological and prenatal, great numbers of people claim the pity shown to a cripple* and the indulgence shown to a child.

There is even a kind of degradation of The Understanding Mind and The Sympathetic Approach. We have our commentators who are not only popularizers but tenderizers; who bring to their task a technique of wise, fatherly appreciation of what's wrong; who anticipate their audience's squawks, who concede in advance the other side of the argument. They are a brand of father-confessor who not simply hears you confess, but, as it were, does your confessing for you. They are a kind of mass-production psychiatrist who ministers to human ills and trials on a least-common-denominator basis. What with the people who have invaded men's privacy, and those who now dispose of men's problems, we have a pretty neat symbolism

---

* The physical cripple has more and more rejected all such special consideration as the mental cripple and pseudocripple have come more and more to demand it.

of modern life: the Age of Publicity merged with the Age of Anxiety, the Peeping Tom's keyhole and the psychoanalyst's couch. It is interesting to note how both activities have widened and spread: how the gossip columnist, beginning with Broadway, Hollywood, Café Society, front-page names, now penetrates into every avenue of politics, into all the arts, and not only circulates gossip but is often first with the news; how the mass-audience adviser holds forth on baseball or burlesque shows, bebop or science fiction, showing how nimbly he can get down-to-earth as well as down-to-bedrock.

And to make an end, there is the matter of the Great Books and Dr. Hutchins and Professor Mortimer Adler and all their co-workers. Here, rather than a vulgarity born of sloppy thinking and materialistic aims—and presumably in answer to it—is something almost brazenly inhuman. Here, rather than a culture that cheapens, softens, adulterates all it touches, is one that desiccates and ossifies. Where all was mush, here all is medicine; where the approach was all cajolery and high-pressuring, here all is intimidation and highhandedness. Instead of the salesman obsequiously out to please, we have the savant who scarcely deigns to advise; where was Beautyrest is now a bed of spikes—and of Procrustes, into the bargain. Instead of culture made-to-measure or altered to fit, here is one suit of armor for all. But no point-by-point analysis of the Great Books could better Mr. Dwight Macdonald's review of them in *The New Yorker*.

The Great Books have about them much more, I feel sure, than mere snob appeal: they have a kind of dim religious light, a sense of the Serious Call, of the medieval scholar-saint. But plainly—if we but keep in mind, say, *The Reader's Digest*—they are once again that mere reversible raincoat of American culture: of our ability to sell an idea at one extreme as well as at another—to sell it so long as it provides a gimmick; and all the better when that gimmick can be elevated into a gospel. Our two favorite gestures are thumbing the nose and bending the knee; what we do not ridicule, we must reverence; nor is it uncommon for us to reverence under one name what we ridicule under another: a weekday freak becomes a Sunday prophet. How not, with materialism and idealism making a teeter-totter of our lives?

America's two most important intellectual forebears are conceivably Franklin and Emerson. Franklin, however, makes us a little uneasy. Poor Richard is at once too goody-goody and too worldly. He argues the prudential approach to life almost too well: he blends copybook morality with eighteenth-century realism; his is the philosophy of the main chance without the cushioning of the noble motive. The special quality in Franklin is that he foreshadowed, with his philistine counsel, what America was to become, while indicating, through his own unflinching worldliness, what it would cease to be. The better, the more central, the more congenial spokesman was Emerson, whose gift for giving a special emphasis and elevation to words has offered us a method for sliding over or circumventing things; whose fine aphorisms are the ancestors, at times even the blood brothers, of our trade-marks and slogans; whose own transcendental visions coagulated or curdled into a great variety of mystical con-games; and whose deep concern for ideas could be made a kind of evasion of realities. Unlike Poor Richard, Emerson doesn't show us up—nor for that matter, pin us down. He is genuinely great without being uncomfortably specific. It is all grand, affirmative, inspiring—yet humorous at moments as well: the sermon without the sinner's bench, the goals without the penalties.

But more significant, even, than our having but two gestures, than our shuttling between extremes of cynicism and idealism, is the fact of extremism, of excessiveness, itself. We conform to so excessive a degree that our very conformity constitutes excess. Our thirsts are so fierce and compulsive that our tastes must necessarily be few and standardized. What we must come to understand is that we cannot remold our culture on any basis of spiritual values applied like a poultice, or of psychiatric treatment distributed, like a papal benediction, to whole multitudes, to an entire society. The conflicts go too deep; the governing impetus, the ruling force, has by now too much momentum. Before we can change direction we must slacken speed; before we can properly treat our organic ailments we must **do s**omething about our nationally mounting high-blood pressure. People are not easily changed, but they are often effectively scared. Could America be induced to start tapering off, the very therapy might consume a part of the disease; for what is wrong with us is less any particular forms of excess than excessiveness itself. And we have aggravated this general extremism by the gods we have made of specific extremes—by our worship of size, by our passion for speed, by our mania for change—by our always scrapping last year's, or even last Wednesday's, model; by our constant determination to build higher, fly faster, swim longer—and, it would sometimes seem, die sooner.

So that we must, quite literally, moderate our ways before we can begin to mend them. So long as immoderacy itself is our weakness, all specific cures can only be transferences: the new faith in God will be as rabid as the old fervor for atheism; the new passion for gardening as intense as the old one for night clubs. And at the moment, so far from having any leaning toward moderation, or even respect for it, we tend to look down on it as a form of mediocrity, a lack of adventurousness, an actual want of aspiration. What we need desperately is ceilings, speed limits, closing hours on most of our ambitions and aims. But that, of course, is precisely the thing we reject: the moderate view is somehow thought to violate spiritual free enterprise. Somehow it isn't the American Way. To be sure it isn't. The American Way is so restlessly creative as to be essentially destructive; the American Way is to carry common sense itself almost to the point of madness.